I hope you enjoy the book!

Chris Davis MD

COMPASSION
AMIDST THE CHAOS

TALES TOLD BY AN **ER** DOC

CHRISTOPHER DAVIS, MD
with KATHLEEN K. DAVIS, MD

Compassion Amidst the Chaos

© Copyright 2020 by Christopher Davis

ISBN (Print): 978-1-09834-069-8
ISBN (eBook): 978-1-09834-070-4

Table of Contents

Moving on: The Pacific Northwest

Teaching Emergency Medicine in Africa and Asia

My Last and Favorite Story

Afterword

Dedication

Emergency Department providers are now engaged in the massive struggle against the Covid-19 pandemic. In my long ER career, I have never been exposed to the risk of contracting such a fatal disease or bringing it home to my family. I offer a special salute to these hard-working, dedicated and courageous healthcare professionals and their loved ones as they fight this peril that is unprecedented in modern times.

Prologue

For thirty-plus years, I worked as an emergency medicine physician in a job I loved. Over this time, I cared for well over 100,000 patients. Motivated by my own desire to better understand what it was about Emergency Medicine that made it such a perfect fit for me, I've described in this book a selection of my actual case histories and related experiences. These stories portray the myriad ways I've been able to contribute to my patients' medical needs as well as the emotional impact these experiences have had upon my growth and development as an ER doc and as a human being.

My Emergency Medicine career has been gratifying for many reasons. This book is about those *unusual cases* that I remember in detail many years later. Each of these patients gave me reason to pause and reflect. More specifically, in each of the stories that follow, I have shared a lesson I learned about medicine, empathy, humility and compassion.

Christopher J Davis, MD
Seattle, Washington
August 18, 2020
chrisdavismd@gmail.com

All the names in this book, except where specified as real, have been changed to protect privacy. The dialogue is my best recollection of what was actually said years ago.

Cold Delivery

One early January morning during my last year of emergency medicine residency at the Johns Hopkins University Hospital in Baltimore, a new beginning brought an unusual challenge and reminded me how much this work was the right fit for me.

Outside, brilliant sunshine bathed the city but was accompanied by an icy blast of Northwest wind. The temperature was in the low twenties. The only direct access to the ER was through the ambulance entrance, which had two sliding glass doors. As you might expect, when an ambulance crew brought a patient to the ER, their stretcher and equipment would open both doors simultaneously, flooding the department with a blast of icy air. Howls of protest would erupt throughout the department with demands of "shut the goddamn doors!" I was fortified by a thin polyester vest that I wore under my white coat. I worried about losing the vest to a spurt of blood, but fortunately that never happened.

Outside those emergency doors, the sound of blaring horns signaled the crush of the early morning Baltimore rush hour. Inside the ER, everyone was whining, moaning and groaning about the winter blast. Suddenly, a man entered through those double doors yelling at the top of his lungs. "Hurry! There has been a minor accident at the corner, but a woman is giving birth RIGHT NOW in the back of a taxicab."

Upon hearing this man's cry for help, I crashed my coffee cup onto the desk, grabbed a towel from the rack and ran outside to help. Instantly, I felt a blast of arctic air temperature, but I shrugged it off. I ran along the sidewalk, pumped up and eager to get to the taxi. Ahead of me, half a block away, the drivers of a group of jammed cars were all honking at each other. The bystander who had alerted us to the problem was running ahead of me and pointed to a taxi in the middle of the intersection. The auto accident was a minor fender bender, but loud screams from the back of the taxi clearly directed me to the back seat.

I opened the rear door to the taxi and found a young lady in the agony of late labor. I could see a bulge developing in the groin area of the lady's jeans and it was clear that the baby's birth was imminent. In those days, I always carried a leather holster on my belt. Similar to an electrician's gear kit, my holster, well-worn like an old catcher's mitt, held two surgical clamps and a pair of serrated "trauma" scissors designed to quickly cut through clothing and also a tourniquet in a small, clean plastic bag. Between screams, I announced to her, "I'm Doctor Davis and I'm here to help you." That introduction was necessary as I whipped out my trauma scissors to cut away her blue jeans. Worried that my scissors might cut the baby's scalp, I proceeded delicately and slowly. She screamed, "Hurry! He's out!"

Two more chop-chops from the serrated scissors and her vaginal area was fully exposed. Just a blink of an eye later, the baby was propelled into my hands just as though I were a quarterback receiving a snap from the center. Out popped a gorgeous, full-term baby boy covered with blood and assorted other fluids. I had no suction bulb to aspirate the fluid from his nose and mouth. I was worried until he took a deep breath and let out a cry that rivaled his mom's.

After most vaginal deliveries, the newborn babies are placed in a heated incubator to make sure their temperature does not drop to dangerous levels. Jeeesus! The temperature outside the cab was still in the twenties with a stiff wind blowing. The umbilical cord is the blood vessel that provides the fetus with a rich supply of blood and necessary nutrients. Normally, after a vaginal delivery, the baby should be held at a level lower than the mother for 1–3 minutes. This provides the baby with an additional supply of iron rich blood, which the baby will need to make his own red blood cells. The cold frost on my breath urged me, *Forget the iron. This baby is about to freeze to death!* Immediately after the birth, a rich flow of maternal blood spilled into the taxi. Now the taxi driver was pissed. He was yelling and hollering about what was happening to his car.

I cradled the baby in the towel and reached for the "trauma" scissors that I had tossed onto the rear seat. Fortunately, they were in easy reach. Designed to cut through clothing and not living tissue, they are not sterile. I took two of the curved Kelly surgical clamps out of my holster and applied them to the umbilical cord several inches above the baby's belly. That stopped the blood flow through the cord. His crying was starting to weaken and now I was panicked about the baby dying from the cold. I quickly cut the umbilical cord between the two clamps, thus freeing the baby from mom. Without waiting to rub away the variety of fluids that covered the baby, I wrapped him in the towel and ran for the ER. I ran through red lights, ignored all of the honking cars and ran faster. I sprinted with every ounce of breath I had. As I dashed through the ER doors, I was welcomed by a pediatric delivery team with a warming bassinet. The anesthesiologist gently delivered oxygen to the baby and the team dashed off to the delivery suite. I crashed into the worn-out chair at the desk and started a search for my much-needed cup of coffee.

The obstetrics resident entered the ER and looked around. "Hey guys, where's mom?"

"Oh shit!" I jumped out of the chair, grabbed an ER stretcher and with one of the techs, pushed the stretcher at a run back to the intersection. Cars squirmed to get around the tiny space between the curb and the taxi; they effectively blocked access to that yellow and black vehicle. By this time, fortunately, several paramedics had arrived and were tending to mom in the back of the cab. She was still bleeding but the paramedics had put in an IV and were giving her fluids. With two paramedics at each end, they lifted the stretcher with mom aboard and shuffled their feet sideways to get the stretcher past the blocking cars. The paramedics charged up the gentle hill with mom on the stretcher. A nurse met them at the door and took them to the Labor and Delivery area to reunite mom with her newborn.

About twenty minutes later, the phone rang. I heard a distant voice call out, "Doctor Davis, it's for you. Labor and Delivery is calling." My heart sank. Had the baby died? Had mom bled to death? My mouth was as dry as cotton when I picked up the phone. A nurse who did not give me her name reported, "Dr. Davis, we have good news for you. Both mom and baby are doing well." But then she continued, "I was just asked to call you. Cutting that umbilical cord with a dirty pair of trauma scissors has everybody worried. Have you ever considered carrying sterile scissors with you?" Inside, I was laughing. Giving myself a moment to compose myself, I thanked her for her wise advice and gently hung up. I did not bother to explain that the sharp teeth of trauma scissors will cut through blue jeans whereas surgical scissors will not. For that reason, I had been able to quickly cut an escape hole for the baby.

Heading back to my coffee, which was now as cold as the outside, I gave free reign to my laughter. Two lives saved but I was called out for non-sterile scissors! As every ER doc knows, good care delivered in time always trumps perfect care delivered late. This is the crazy, amazing life that made me so enjoy being an ER doc.

Choosing a Career:
Finding the Right Fit

From MIT to Medical School

How did I find myself rescuing a woman in labor in sub-freezing cold after a traffic accident? For me, it has been a fun and fascinating journey.

I grew up in a Navy family. My dad had been an extremely successful officer in the Navy as a civil engineer. After being imprisoned for forty-two months in a notorious POW camp in Japan during WW II, he remained on active duty and went from lieutenant to becoming a two-star admiral in only fifteen years. I was also fortunate to have a very bright, empathetic mother and three sisters.

Like everyone else, my youth had good news and bad news. Because my dad's career had rocketed so quickly to success, the Navy moved us a lot. In fact, between kindergarten and graduating from high school, I had been enrolled in ten separate schools. The obvious downside of that peripatetic life was that I had made few lasting friendships growing up. As my dad's success had given me a tremendous fear of failure, the two combined to make me quite a nerd. I studied hard and usually had the highest GPA in whatever school I was attending. The other challenge was that my dad-imposed Navy-style discipline upon his kids. That tended to smother out any feelings of levity when he was around. I was never particularly interested in sports until I rowed crew in college so didn't feel I had a lot to offer in male conversations. However, there was plenty of good news. My three sisters taught me that if I asked a lady a question about a topic that she enjoyed, I would learn something new and interesting, and she might even like me!

Science and math had always interested me, and I assumed I would follow that pathway in college. During my senior year in high school, we were stationed in Hawaii where I attended the highly regarded Punahou High School. I was accepted to MIT and, thanks to warm endorsements from Punahou's faculty, Harvard had shown an interest in me. At that time, the Vietnam War was building. The resultant increase in college protests against America's involvement in that conflict deeply angered my admiral father. When we talked about what college I should attend, he made it clear that a liberal arts-based college, such as Harvard, was out of the question. To make his point, he calmly said: "Well Chris, you have a choice. It's MIT or the Marine Corps." I went to MIT.

As school to this point had been rather easy for me, I failed to develop the most crucial elements of academic success: being organized and to not procrastinate. Before going to MIT, I had passed the Advanced Placement course in calculus and so MIT waived that requirement. I decided to take the course again believing that an "A" would be an easy way to start my college career. I got a "C-." Fortunately, I had joined a fine fraternity, Sigma Chi. My fraternity brothers quickly set out to correct my academic behavioral weaknesses and were quite successful. My improvement at MIT was like a freight train getting underway: the improvement was painfully slow but definite.

I enrolled in the mechanical engineering program at MIT, which I found truly interesting. Having grown up in the military, I also was comfortable signing up for the Air Force Reserve Officer Training Corps (AFROTC), as the Air Force offered me a full scholarship. That was terrific—but the devil was in the details. If I failed to graduate from MIT after eight semesters, I would need to repay my scholarship by serving in the Air Force as an enlisted man for four years.

Like so many college students, I was becoming more concerned about the Vietnam War. The photo of a young Vietnamese child running after having been napalmed shocked the world. In those days, careers in mechanical engineering largely meant designing military equipment such as jet fighters. I remember Moshe Dayan's famous comment: "Fighter planes are not washing machines. They are killing machines."

At that point, I started to give serious thought towards becoming a doctor. One afternoon, I had a meeting with the "pre-med" advisor for MIT. She had been amazed at how many students at MIT wanted to go to medical school. Her theory was the same as mine; MIT students were becoming progressively less interested in the military-industrial complex. She suggested that I work as a volunteer in the emergency department of the Boston City Hospital to get a feeling for what it might be like. I took her advice and never looked back.

Ultimately, by my senior year in 1968, I had been I accepted by four medical schools, including the George Washington University School of Medicine in Washington, D.C. My girlfriend, Kathleen, had just graduated from Wellesley and had a job lined up in Cambridge to help with neurological research at Harvard. By this time, I had racked up six months of being America's most love-sick puppy. The thought of Kathleen working at Harvard filled me with anxiety of astronomical dimensions. As GW was located only a short plane ride to Boston, I chose GW's medical school. GW turned out to be a terrific choice for me.

Now, I want to take you back to my sophomore year at MIT and Boston City Hospital.

Lessons as an ER Volunteer: Boston City Hospital

I wore my first student white coat one night in Boston City Hospital in October 1965. The ID tag on the coat lapel displayed my name hastily written with a leaky ballpoint pen: *C. Davis, Volunteer.* I was nervous. Everyone in the ER assumed that as a college student volunteer, I had no idea what I was supposed to do. The charge nurse kept a close eye on me.

The Boston City Hospital ER in those days was small and dimly lit by overhead fluorescent bulbs. The new patients waiting to be "clocked in" were sitting in a row along the corridor. At the end of the corridor was a metal desk, labeled "triage", where I took their "histories." My job was to enter on the chart the patient's name, address, age, sex and a brief description of why they had come to the ER. At the bottom was one line on which was printed: PMH, Meds, Allergies. The charge nurse explained to me that PMH meant "past medical history." It was less overwhelming for me that all the patients that I saw had been healthy enough to walk in with sore throats, an injured arm, cough, etc. After an hour or so, I thought that my responsibilities were not so scary after all. After I had completed each patient's history form, I walked a few steps down the somewhat dingy corridor to the charge nurse's desk where I placed each chart in a black metal bin.

The charge nurse's name as I recall was Murphy. This being Boston, Irish names were very common. She was short, 5'2" at most, with long hair stacked on top of her head as was the style back then.

"Ms. Murphy, do you ever have a problem with violent people coming through the front door? I mean, you are sitting right near the front door."

She grinned at me and hopped off her high chair. She reached into the side of her desk and pulled out an enormous "nightstick," the kind of club police officers carry. "I've never actually been in danger," she said with a smile. She quickly returned the weapon to the inside of her desk in hopes that the patients had failed to notice it.

According to the chart, one of my patients was a man in his early 60s complaining of diarrhea. I called out the name on the chart, George Jones. He was seated in the hallway next to the triage desk. This small, tired Black man slowly stood up and shuffled over and sat down.

I asked, "George, what seems to be the problem?"

He replied, "I got diarrhea real bad."

Being a medical neophyte, that didn't seem to me like such a huge problem that would require him to come to the ER on a Saturday night. I asked him additional questions, but I was uncomfortable getting the history within earshot of the long line of patients waiting to be seen along the hall.

He went on to explain, "I drive a garbage truck. My job is to lift the trash into the back of the truck. But yesterday, I had watery shits every hour. Lifting a heavy trash can when you feel that your bowels are about to blow up is powerful (sic) awful. I had to stop lots of times to go. I was very late finishing my route. My boss was mad."

Being a hopeless rookie, I did not know what questions to ask. Was I supposed to ask if he had chills, fever or if he had abdominal pain? There were many symptoms that I should have asked about had I really understood what I was doing. Moments later, one of the Boston University medical residents picked up George Jones' chart and invited him back to a small treatment area while I proceeded to interview the next patient.

After George had been seen by one of the doctors, one of the second-year medical residents took me aside and said, "Don't worry about getting the clinical history. If you do, you will slow us down. Just name, address and complaint. That's all. We'll do the rest." That helped. Once I realized that my job was only clerical, I felt less nervous.

After George Jones had received his prescription and was ready to leave, he motioned to me with his hand to come over so that he could speak to me.

He craned his neck back to read my name tag. "Hmm. Davis. Volunteer. What are you doing here?"

"I'm just trying to help out. I think that I might want to go to medical school, so I am here to learn."

"Hmm." He replied again. "Are you in school now?"

"Yes. I am an engineering student at MIT."

He paused, again. "You are obviously a smart boy and you might have a bright future ahead of you. But I am worried that you just might be a failure in life."

I was startled. I asked, "What do you mean?"

He straightened himself up to his full height and quietly growled, "I mean, son, that getting by in the world is all about respect. You called me George. To you, I am not George. I am Mr. George Jones. Ya got it? If you want to be respected as a doctor, you first gotta learn to treat your patients with respect."

At first, I felt defensive. However, a quick reflection on how hard this man's life was from day to day gave me pause. This was a man for whom nothing had come easily. To him, I was a privileged, white collegiate brat. But it occurred to me that he was not saying this to put me down. He took the time to say this because, in a wonderful way, he seemed to care about me.

During most of my early years growing up in a Navy family, the only Black person I had ever known was our cleaning lady when we lived in Virginia named Josephine. She was warm and kind. We loved her as a very close friend; my parents, sisters and I always addressed her as Josephine without giving it any other thought.

When I was in fifth grade in 1955 and attending a Catholic elementary school in Virginia, I was in the nurse's office for some minor problem. In the next room, I heard a Black couple talking with the priest who was the principal of the school. The Black couple wanted to enroll their child, but I heard the principal say that he could not do that because if he did, lots of the white parents would pull their children out of the school.

I told my dad that night of the encounter and he was livid. At the end of the school year, he pulled me out and sent me to the public school.

My dad had grown up in poverty but escaped his impoverished childhood thanks to the U.S. Naval Academy where he graduated in 1934. His WW II experiences, including three years in a notorious POW camp in Tokyo, honed his courage, honesty and fairness. Certainly, he was more troubled by racial injustice than the average citizen of Virginia in 1955.

In our house, in keeping with the Navy tradition of formal courtesy, I was taught to address everyone as "Sir", "Ma'am" or "Miss." Our cleaning lady, however, was just plain old Josephine. Immediately, I thought of Josephine and then it hit me. Like it or not, I had addressed Mr. Jones as George because I thought that was the socially appropriate thing to do; you called Black adults by their first name—simply Josephine. But now I suddenly wondered, "Why in the hell if I had addressed white people by a title, was I addressing Black people by their first name?" As I glanced down the hall to the sitting patients waiting to be seen, I noticed that most were Black. As my mother used to say, "What would Jesus do?" If I was going to take care of countless Black people in my future as a doctor, I'd better grow up. George was right; it is all about being respectful.

The manner in which Blacks were treated in 1965 made me wonder if the Nazis lived on. The previous summer, I had been on vacation in Europe visiting my sister and her husband, a naval officer assigned to Naples. Late one afternoon in Brussels, I was walking down the sidewalk taking in the sights. I noticed a small crowd that had collected in front of a store. I went over to investigate. In the front window of the store was a large television. On the TV, the station was showing clips of Black people in the South of the United States in civil rights marches. Enormous, vicious German Shepherds were biting and slashing the unprotected Black marchers. The police held the dogs on a leash—a leash just long enough to allow the dogs to bite and tear into the flesh of their selected targets. Another scene showed a high-powered water cannon hosing down a small group of young Black marchers. The marchers were being knocked onto the concrete. They were crying, screaming and trying to crawl away. The Belgians watching the TV were silent but would individually let out gasps of shock and anger. I felt nauseated. For the first time, I felt ashamed to be an American. Slowly, being careful to not say anything to anyone that would identify me as an American, I slipped away.

These televised scenes of biting dogs and fire hoses aimed at marchers as well as my encounter with Mr. George Jones made a huge impact on me. For the rest of my adult life, I employed the formalized courtesy of my military upbringing to address every adult of any color as "Mr." or a "Ma'am" or a "Miss".

Later, the same evening in the ER, I was near the entrance when the outside doors flew open. A huge man staggered in soaked in sweat, crying out, "I can't breathe! I can't breathe!" The doctors and nurses helped the gasping man onto a stretcher, sat him upright, applied an oxygen mask and started an IV. The mask was delivering oxygen so fast that a cloud of water vapor rose from the patient's face.

Two second-year Boston University medical residents rushed to his side. With the doctors standing on opposite sides of the patient, they lifted his shirt and listened to the back of his chest with their stethoscopes. After moving their stethoscopes in different directions across his back, they both looked at each other and nodded.

"Pulmonary edema," said one resident.

"Agreed," said the other.

Turning to speak directly to the patient, one resident asked, "Mr. Bayles, do you have chest pain?"

The patient shook his head but was too short of breath to talk.

The nurse reported, "BP 175/120, pulse 110, respirations about 30."

"Francine, please give Mr. Bayles..." then there followed a long string of medication orders that meant nothing to me.

After specifying these orders, the resident concluded, "The EKG shows no acute changes. Also, the fact that he doesn't have chest pain is reassuring. But he still needs a bed in the Coronary Care Unit."

One of the residents remained at his bedside constantly for the next hour. The tech put a tube into his penis and a flood of urine came out and drained into a bag. After a few minutes, the oxygen seemed to be helping him and he appeared less desperate to breathe. Mr. Bayles was hooked up to an EKG and the resident studied the results in careful detail. He commented to the other doctor something about there being "no apparent heart attack."

When one of the nurses had a free moment, I asked her what was going on. First, she scanned the scene to make sure that there wasn't something more important to do than talk to me. Reassured, she said, "He's got pulmonary edema. That's a situation where the pumping action of the heart is so weak that the blood backs up into the lungs. Fluid leaks out of the blood vessels and floods the air sacs. That prevents oxygen from getting into the blood vessels. It's sort of like a plugged-up drain pipe. The fluid gets backed up until the correct therapy drains it out of the lungs so that oxygen can finally get in. Pretty cool, huh?"

I witnessed what seemed to me to be a miracle; Mr. Bayles gradually improved. After about an hour, he was alert and talking to his wife. Since the crisis had passed, I approached the stretcher and spoke to the patient.

"How are you doing?" I asked.

The patient smiled at me, gave thumbs up and said, "I'm just thanking the Lord that he got me here in time. You doctors are somethin' else." He reached over and clasped my hand, cheerfully oblivious to the fact that I had done nothing to help him.

But his experience helped me. These two medical residents had saved this man's life like it was a routine matter. They didn't even have the time to enjoy the overwhelming satisfaction of having done so because they were already busy with other patients. Clearly, for them, it was just part of the job. I'd learned a significant reality about the ER role.

Mr. Bayles' medical condition also helped me make an important connection to my own studies. As the nurse described it, this problem was analogous to a malfunctioning pump. This man had a problem with poor pump function, which caused back pressure to force fluid where it should not go. He improved when the fluid was drained, and he received pressurized oxygen and medicine to enable his heart to beat more strongly. An insight dawned on me; these doctors were using many of the principles of mechanical engineering to save this man's life! OMG! How cool is that? I felt excited and more certain the ER might be my future career path.

All of the residents were from the Boston University Medical Center training program. Polite, kind, hard-working and efficient, they were very welcoming to me—me who was a next to worthless volunteer. In one evening, they had become my new professional role models.

By five in the morning, the ER had quieted down. Only a few patients remained to be seen and I was tired—it was time to go home. Boston City Hospital was located in Roxbury, which was almost an exclusively Black community. Like many such inner-city neighborhoods, poverty and crime cast a long shadow over its residents. I left the ER and started the long walk down Massachusetts Avenue back to my fraternity house on Beacon Street in Boston's Back Bay neighborhood. The street was basically deserted, and sunrise was still two hours away.

As I crossed at one intersection, I found myself abruptly surrounded by five young Black males in their late teens. The street light barely illuminated their faces. They had surrounded me in unison and in complete silence.

"Hey white boy, what'cha doin' here?" said the tallest one. I was scared silly.

"I'm just going home." George Jones' clarion call to treat everyone with respect rang in my head like Big Ben.

"But what'cha doin' here? It's late, ya' know. Say man, are you prejudiced against Black folks?"

"No. Why?" At this point, I felt like I was shaking like a leaf in a hurricane.

"C'mon man. You're white. What have you got against us Black folks?"

By this time, it was obvious that I was scared. At least two of the guys were standing right behind me—very close.

Again, he asked, "Aren't you prejudiced against us Black people? After all, you're white. All whites hate us."

"Not me. That's why I am here." I replied.

"Come again? Are you just messin' with us or what?"

"No. I'm just heading home after working at the hospital. In the emergency department."

"Oh yeah? Why would you want to do that?"

"Well, I want to be a doctor. The ER teaches me good stuff and gives me a chance to help out in the neighborhood."

"Oh yeah. Like what?"

I described what I had seen and how wonderful I thought it was that these doctors and nurses were helping so many people in Roxbury even late on a Saturday night.

"Did you see any Black doctors?"

"Yes, two." I lied.

What followed was an amazing conversation with these five street teens about the ER and how it was there 24/7 to help the people of Roxbury.

"Well, OK, man. Be cool. But if you are smart enough to be a doctor, you should be smart enough to not be out here at five in the morning."

I extended my hand. He looked surprised—then gave me a warm hand-shake. I took his advice. I never again left the ER until after sunrise.

The ER of Boston City Hospital in 1965 was an open theater of clinical medicine. A rookie like me could wander about unsupervised to talk, listen and learn. I often had a box seat as I watched doctors diagnose one mysterious set of symptoms after another. As it turned out, it was also an important teaching milieu about the critical ingredient of respect and its relevance to my future as a medical provider. The curtain came down on that marvelous learning laboratory when a new ER medical director took over and tightened the ship. That ER is no longer an open learning laboratory. To experience anything like that nowadays, one would need to get specific training as a volunteer. For me, this opportunity focused me toward medical school as my goal.

Medical Training: An intellectual Roller Coaster

I graduated from MIT in 1968 and entered medical school at the George Washington University in Washington, D.C. From the very start, I enjoyed medical school, as I now felt that I was on the right track towards a promising career. Immediately, I recognized that the learning process was quite different from engineering school.

I had a rocky start. I did poorly on my first anatomy exam. Embarrassed, I went to talk to the anatomy professor to get his advice. In a rather tactless way, I asked, "Do you mean that I have to *memorize* all this anatomical detail?"

With a smile and the patience acquired from years of teaching, he explained, "Chris, you are experiencing what most graduates from engineering schools experience when they start medical school. In engineering, if you understand the math, the math can take you just about wherever you need to go. Medicine is different and is built on pattern recognition where the roadmap of math is much less applicable." This issue troubled me a great deal. Memorizing seemed to me to be such a primitive way to learn. But as I thought about it, I realized that memorizing anatomical detail is a rigorous way to train your memory. Memorization requires focused concentration.

Thinking about my visit to the Louvre in Paris a few years earlier, I suddenly saw a connection between learning about art and learning medicine. I said to myself, *Chris, imagine that you are studying art in a huge gallery. Math won't help you much here. Building your knowledge is about understanding the similarities and differences among hundreds of paintings. This analogy applies to medicine. Being a physician is about understanding the similarities and differences among hundreds of patients. I realized then that memorizing medical information would provide the background to be able to make medical comparisons between patients while simultaneously improving my ability to focus and concentrate on the vast amount of information I would be required to learn.*

I enjoyed the collaborative learning that is a hallmark of medical school. In the anatomy lab, I dissected a cadaver with three other students. On visiting the patients during the rounds in the wards, I participated as a member of a team. Case discussions with the residents required me to be on top of the topic in order to contribute to the discussion. I quickly developed a respect for how much I could learn listening to my classmates. We rotated through frequently changing teams, which allowed me to get to know and work with virtually every one of the 100 students in my medical school class.

After my first year, I married Kathleen, a woman whose qualities vastly exceeded what I had pictured as the lady of my dreams. I was a happy fellow.

After graduation, I signed up for one year of internship at the George Washington University Hospital prior to entering the Air Force for three years as required by my ROTC obligation. Internship year consisted of a series of rotations in different parts of medicine. I enjoyed them all with a huge exception. I hated my two months of rotation in the ER.

The role of an emergency department in a teaching hospital like George Washington University is complex. In addition to providing timely care for the patients, it must offer suitable and effective training for interns and residents. In 1973, the system did not work as well as needed.

The physical set-up of the GW Hospital ER initially looked promising. Each patient room was isolated from its neighbor by a wood and glass wall. The nurses' station was located right in the geometric center of the facility. Best of all, there was a huge white board above the nurses' station that kept a running record as to which patient needed to go to x-ray, get medications, needed a laceration sutured or was ready to go home.

But it soon became woefully clear that the ER facility and its management were barely adequate for the number of patients seeking care. At this time, the demand for emergency medical care was soaring across the country. The physical size of the ER was too small, and the patients waited too long to be seen. Moving patients through the ER proceeded at glacial speed because each patient during his/her visit was usually seen by multiple providers. These might include medical students, an intern or possibly residents from a specialty. Incoming cases were assigned according to the presenting "chief complaint." Chest pain went to the medical intern, while abdominal pain went to the surgical intern, but there was usually a mix-and-match adjustment depending on the patient load.

For example, I had a case of a young female patient who came with right lower quadrant pain. Her story and examination were suggestive of both appendicitis and an ectopic pregnancy. After my evaluation, I called the gynecology team. Their responding intern, who was as unqualified in gynecology as I was, took a message and went to tell his resident. In this particular case, I got a call back saying the team was going to the OR for a Cesarean section after which they had to make rounds, as they were behind. The clock continued to tick, tick, tick… After what seemed like an interminable delay, the team showed up in the ER. By this time, the patient was feeling much better and her pain had largely subsided. Part of the reason that I remember this case so well is that the team resident was pissed off at me for wasting his time. The resident snarled at me saying, "If you guys down here in the ER had the vaguest idea of how to take care of patients, I wouldn't need to be always rushing down here." Impolite though he was to me, I knew he was right.

I did not feel qualified to be working in the ER without close instruction and supervision. The problem was not just GW's. Medical schools across the country had not yet developed training programs to turn residents into knowledgeable, well-qualified and experienced emergency medicine physicians.

In addition to the lack of supervision and specialized medical skills for this ER role, I was not prepared emotionally to confront how rapidly patients can die in the ER. One night, I experienced my first life-threatening trauma case. I was the medical intern when the ambulance team brought in a tall muscular police officer on a stretcher. While riding his motorcycle through an intersection in D.C., the officer was "T- boned" by the driver of a pickup truck who had run a red light. The impact catapulted the officer into the air, and he landed on a cement curb. The driver of the truck sped away.

Upon his arrival in the ER, the officer was whisked to the trauma room, a special room for such cases. Fortunately, it was empty at that moment. The hospital PA system shouted, "Surgical team to the ER STAT." After a minute or two, the chief surgical resident and his team arrived in the ER to care for this dying man. The surgical residents quickly went about their business: starting IV fluids, cutting off clothes, applying an oxygen mask and making their initial assessments.

I had never seen a major trauma before and so I stood near the head of the patient's stretcher. Just then, the patient reached over and grabbed the lapel of my white coat and pleaded, "Doc, don't let me die! Please don't let me die! I've got a wife and three kids. Please don't let me die!" In less than one hour, he was dead. I was crushed. Even though I was not part of the surgical team trying to save him and had no training or talent to care for this man, he thought I was one of his doctors. He was counting on me to save him. Logically, I had nothing to do with his death, but emotionally I was devastated. I was convinced that somehow, I had let him down. After the end of my shift, I sat in my car—waiting for the tears to stop. As I write this now, some forty years later, the melancholy returns. At the time, my grief quickly turned to fury. I was repeatedly struck during the surgical team's post-mortem discussion and the police department's follow-up investigation by how this loss was treated in such a cool, matter-of-fact manner. No one seemed to register shock, horror, or a sense of loss, except me. I hated the ER more than ever. I couldn't wait to get out of there and never return.

After completing my internship, I reported to the Air Force. I volunteered to be a flight surgeon. Flight surgeons are physicians provided with extra training to enable them to take medical care of flight crews. Part of that job was to fly regularly with those air crews. By knowing the details of the job of each crew member, a flight surgeon could make an intelligent decision as to who needed to be grounded until a medical problem could be fixed versus those who were OK to return to flying status. I had a very positive experience in the Air Force. I found that the personnel were smart, well trained and very professional. They demonstrated a commitment to excellence and courtesy toward each other, which was an integral part of their culture.

One afternoon in the autumn of 1974, while having lunch in the Andrews AFB hospital cafeteria, I had a chance encounter with a friend of mine named Dr. Phil Buttaravoli (real name). Phil was striding past when he spotted me and set his tray down on the small table I had chosen over by the wall of windows. "Hey Phil, good to see you. Please join me," I said. I had known Phil for only a few months. We had met at an Air Force meeting and hit it off quickly. He looked like a runner or a tennis player in great shape with a trim physique. I had forgotten that he was the director of the emergency department at the Andrews AFB hospital. Phil was a Major and graduate of the emergency residency program at the University of Cincinnati.

In the early 1970s, the University of Cincinnati was the first of only a few medical schools in the United States to realize that the training for emergency medicine doctors throughout the country was inadequate. Medical schools were only beginning to insist that ER docs needed to be trained to the same level of focused knowledge and clinical wisdom as internists, surgeons and every other physician specialty. Perhaps ER training was improving because hospital administrators were also concerned about the howling protests from patients complaining about poor care and the malpractice risks inherent in the current regimen.

As we gulped down our lunch, and after we had spent a few minutes getting caught up on our lives, I asked, "Phil, I hated my ER time. How do you stand it?" I then told him in graphic detail how emotionally devastated I had been by the tragedy of the motorcycle police officer.

As he leaned closer, Phil nodded and said, "I hear you, Chris. I went through the same process of feeling physically, emotionally and intellectually crushed by life in the ER." Sitting up straighter, Phil continued, "What I love is that in the ER, you are not a one-organ doctor. You need to have a good grasp of virtually all of clinical medicine. The intellectual challenge is enormous. Remember, you are often the guy who prevents death NOW."

Shaking his head slowly, Phil added, "ERs in this country are a mess and are in desperate need of doctors with the skill set and the guts to stop tragedy in its tracks. That poor cop's death could inspire you to save hundreds more." His face lit up as he continued, "Come on, Chris, in how many other jobs do you have the chance to save lives virtually every day? Besides, look at you. You love to fly in high performance Air Force jet fighters. Like me, you are an action junkie at heart. Chris, think about it," he said gently slapping my shoulder, "this may actually be your calling."

Phil stood up then and we both headed back to our jobs. That evening, I went jogging at the local high school track. As I reflected on Phil's comments, I thought about how I had been considering becoming a cardiologist. But as he had cautioned, did I want to be a one-organ system specialist? I realized that in the Air Force, I had enjoyed the wide variety of medical problems I had to treat. Maybe a diverse group of patients with critical issues would suit me better.

Phil Buttaravoli's recommendation that I take a careful look at ER medicine and how I could help improve it turned out to be the most important professional advice I have ever received.

I understood then that the reason I hated the ER was because I was inadequately trained and had too much responsibility for someone with so little experience. But doing an emergency medicine residency would change all that. I felt that Phil was right about me. I would love the challenges he outlined and the chance to save lives in a milieu that guaranteed action and a high level of responsibility.

In those days, there were very few emergency medicine residencies. My wife was in training at the George Washington University School of Medicine in Washington, D.C., my alma mater. I needed to find an ER residency that would fit with my family life. Fortunately, Johns Hopkins in nearby Baltimore had started such a residency a few years before. I was accepted and entered the Hopkins program one month after my discharge from the Air Force in 1976.

Addendum: Now in 2020, the medical director of the emergency department at the George Washington University Medical Center, Dr. Rob Shesser (real name), has built a top-flight, eagerly sought-after ER residency program at George Washington University Hospital in Washington, D.C.

Serving and Adventure: USAF, Iceland

Flight Surgeon

For my first two years in the Air Force, I was stationed at the Andrews AFB flight medicine office.

My dad, a career naval officer, had always said, "The Air Force takes better care of their people than any other service." I experienced a striking example of this Air Force consideration for their personnel shortly after I began my service. My first assignment in the Air Force was to go to Kunsan, Korea. I called the officer who makes assignments and asked him if, after my one year in Korea, I could come back to Andrews AFB in Washington, D.C. to be near my wife's medical school. He said, "I don't know. I do not foresee any vacancies at Andrews when you return from Korea. Let me take a look." One week later, there was a FedEx package on my doorstep. The officer had cancelled my orders to Korea and changed them to Andrews AFB. Delighted, I called to thank him. He appreciated the call and said, "I believe that if you and your wife are happy, you will do a better job for the Air Force." That was the most enlightened HR philosophy I had ever heard.

At that time, about one-third of all the USAF flight surgeons were stationed overseas. By 1975, it was my turn; I was assigned to Iceland. As a flight surgeon in Iceland, I enjoyed diverse opportunities and responsibilities. My job included helping the general surgeon with his abdominal operations, assisting the orthopedist in setting fractures, delivering babies and caring for pediatric cases. But it also enabled me to routinely fly in high speed fighter jets, assist in rescue missions, determine the flying status of pilots before and after an accident or injury, meet with senior officers about squadron issues, and even give advice to crews over the radio dealing with an unexpected problem.

Keflavik, Iceland, is a small fishing village at the end of a bleak, rock strewn peninsula projecting into the North Atlantic Sea. In 1975, I was in my third and final year of Air Force service as a flight surgeon prior to entering my emergency medicine residency. I was assigned to the Keflavik NATO air base as an "unaccompanied tour," meaning that my wife could not join me. The base was actually controlled by the U.S. Navy but hosted the Air Force flying squadrons as "tenants." The hospital was entirely staffed with Navy physicians and surgeons. I was the only Air Force doctor assigned to the staff. In this environment of cold, high winds and frequent fog, Keflavik fishermen brave the elements in small boats to harvest fish in the manner of their ancestors. The natural beauty of Iceland is breathtaking, and the Icelandic heritage and culture fascinated me.

The job of a flight surgeon is first and foremost to provide medical care to flight crews. Due to the often-stressful situations that air crews encounter, the flight surgeon must know, in addition to routine out-patient medicine, the details of the man-machine environment in the aircraft. The flight surgeon has the responsibility to "ground" a crew member who is not well enough to fly and, therefore, needs intimate knowledge of each member's job to make appropriate flying status decisions. This can be tricky. If it were necessary to ground a pilot who was scheduled to begin an important mission, this decision might create immense resentment towards the flight surgeon. Since I lived in the same dormitory as the flight crews, I had opportunities to cultivate warm, cordial relations with them; this helped me establish and maintain their trust.

A flight surgeon's job requires him to routinely fly in all the aircraft flown by each of his crews. While there is always extra room in the cockpit of a transport helicopter, the jet fighter situation is quite different. The jet fighter associated with our detachment was the famous F-4 Phantom. Just parked on the ramp, the Phantom looked like a bull that was already pissed off. For its time, the Phantom had no competition as the most capable and deadly fighter for the Navy, Air Force, Marine Corps and many of our allies. It weighed 55,000 pounds fully loaded. The vast majority of that weight consisted of fuel, bombs or rockets and two jet engines turning 7,500 RPM. What I loved was that the Phantom had only two seats—one for the pilot and behind him, a seat for the Weapons Systems officer (WSO). So, in order to qualify to fly in the rear seat as the WSO, the Air Force put me through a crash course in how to operate the radar, the navigation systems and prepare the weapons for launch by the pilot. In addition, the AF sent me to Florida for water survival school on the assumption that if I ejected over the cold North Atlantic, I had better know what to do to survive.

Our F-4 squadron was charged with protecting Icelandic airspace from Russian intruders, so we practiced air-to-air intercepts. Operating the radar looking for "targets" while charging through the air doing tight turns, steep climbs, twists and dives at hundreds of miles per hour challenged every neuron in my brain. After two missions, I overcame any airsickness and thereafter loved every minute of it.

Flight Emergency

In January of 1976, I faced a crisis. Most of the crews had returned from Christmas leave and members were teasing each other about how "rusty" their flying had become. January flying weather in Iceland has always been notoriously poor but on this day the sky occasionally displayed brief patches of blue. I was in my office seeing patients when my portable radio sounded.

"Doc, the squadron commander needs you down here now. We've got a no shit F-4 emergency." I jumped in my ancient VW Bug and went streaking down to the flight line.

Panting from my sprint from the car, I met the squadron commander whose name was Harold "Bull" Brock. "What's the problem colonel?"

"It's Byron Cahill in Sloe Gin 53. He says his oxygen is making him sick and he thinks that he might have to eject."

A lightning bolt of alarm lit up my brain. If the two-man crew ejected, they would certainly land on the huge rock piles that surrounded the field or they would parachute into the Atlantic with its 32-degree water temperature. Worse was the thought of what the airplane would do if it crashed. If the airplane went down into the nearby Icelandic village of Keflavik, many lives would be lost. If it circled back and crashed into the base, an equally devastating disaster would occur.

I picked up the radio and called Sloe Gin 53.

"Byron, this is the flight surgeon. What's happening?"

"Hey doc, we are in deep shit. I think the oxygen tank is bad. When I try to breathe, it seems like I am getting no air."

As he spoke, I could hear over the radio the sounds of him taking deep, rapid breaths. He was clearly breathing too fast and too deeply. But why?

"Byron, do you have any numbness of tingling in your hands?" I asked.

"Yeah doc, I can barely feel the throttle or the joystick." His fast, heavy breathing continued to be audible over the radio.

"Byron, do you have any tightness in your chest or around your ribs?"

"Jeeeesus doc, I feel like there is a tight belt around my chest. That's why I feel I cannot get enough air."

Byron was an experienced and decorated fighter pilot with numerous combat sorties during the Vietnam War. Byron was not the sort of pilot to panic. Nevertheless, he was having a panic attack!

The diagnosis was clear. Byron was suffering from Acute Hyperventilation Syndrome. Normally, this is scary to the patient, but is easily corrected in the office or the ER. However, this pilot was terrified and the thought of what his crashing airplane might do scared us all. Stress causes this Syndrome. In a situation where a person feels anxious, sometimes he will breathe faster and deeper than is necessary. This is part of the "fight or flight" response. As the person breathes faster and deeper than he needs to, he exhales too much carbon dioxide. The chemical receptors in the arteries in the neck realize that the person is over-breathing and try to slow down the process. The brain sends signals to the breathing muscles in the chest to try to slow things down. Unfortunately, the patient feels this contraction of the chest wall muscles, which makes breathing harder. Often, this makes his panic worse. When the patient's carbon dioxide in the blood gets too low, it causes a temporary drop in the amount of calcium in the blood. This calcium drop then causes numbness and tingling in the hands and face, which is scary too.

"Byron, this is what I want you to do. Take off your mask, slow down to under 180 knots and crack your canopy open just a bit. That will get you off the oxygen and breathing sea level air and you will start to feel better—quickly."

"OK, doc. Here goes." A few seconds later, I heard the roar in the cockpit of the rapid flow of air as he took off his oxygen mask. The mask contained his radio mike so now it was hard to hear him. In the meantime, Byron was orbiting the field; he had attracted the attention of dozens of onlookers. The squadron commander mobilized the fire trucks to handle a potential crash. I winced when I saw this, as I was concerned that this would make Byron's panic worse.

A few moments later, Byron was back on the radio. I could hear him more clearly than before. "Hey doc, that sea level air tastes mighty good."

Realizing that he was talking to me having put his mask back on to use the radio, I growled at him. 'Byron, I copy you loud and clear. Did you put your mask back on?"

"Yeah, yeah." The return of the background noise convinced me that his mask was off again as I had ordered.

The squadron commander picked up the mike. Before he said anything, I cautioned him to not ask, "Are you feeling better," but to say, "Are things going any better now?"

"Yes, sir. I am feeling pretty good now."

Byron was cleared to land and did so without any problems. The WSO in the back seat was both relieved and pissed. Since the WSO said that he had no problem with the oxygen, a credibility shadow started to settle on Byron. I took him back to our modest ER and determined that Byron was fine now.

Afterwards, Bull Brock called me into his office. His aircraft maintenance chief was already there when I arrived. Brock growled, "Doc, if our oxygen source is bad, every goddamn plane here will need to be grounded until the problem is fixed with a new supply of oxygen and until we have the systems inspected and re-certified." With a quick stroke, he crashed his fist down onto the desk. He bellowed, "Doc, I would like you to sit in Byron's F-4, breathe that stuff and tell me if you think it has been poisoned."

My body quickened with the chance to be a doc/detective hero. I thought, *Wow! Great idea! But on second thought, uh oh, holy shit!*

With a somewhat wobbly salute, I left to go to the hangar where the F-4 was parked. I climbed into the pilot's seat and sniffed the mask. It seemed OK.

After snapping the mask to my helmet, I turned on the oxygen tanks. Byron had climbed into the back seat and was breathing the same oxygen I was. Byron and I exchanged reassuring chatter over the intercom when something odd started to happen. I found myself taking deeper breaths more rapidly. It wasn't long until my hands started to tingle and weaken my grip. A few minutes later, I started to feel a belt around my chest, and I struggled to get enough air in.

"Good Lord. I am getting Acute Hyperventilation Syndrome too."

Byron called from the back seat "How are you doin', doc?" It was immediately clear to me that he could hear my fast, deep breathing though the cockpit intercom. He knew what was happening to me.

Then it occurred to me that I was hyperventilating too because I was afraid that I was breathing poisoned oxygen. I was just as full of fear as Byron had been. However, in the backseat, Byron was feeling fine. I asked him to tell me about his Christmas leave so that I could use my watch to dial down my breathing rate. After 45 minutes, both Byron and I were convinced that the oxygen system was OK.

The Bull was clearly pleased that everything was OK. But then he asked, "Doc, what causes this Hyper...whatever you call it and what should a fellow do about it?"

After I had reviewed the physiology of hyperventilation, I recommended that in a serene setting, it would be important to reassure the patient, and to explain what is happening. Breathing in and out through a brown paper bag would also help.

"What should an F-4 jock do if this were to happen to him?"

I explained that the pilot must first understand what is happening, abort the mission, and if possible, drop to a low enough altitude so that he can admit sea level air into the cockpit. I added that among fighter pilots, Hyperventilation Syndrome is rarely a problem during the turmoil of combat but is more likely to occur in the period of anticipation before a particularly dangerous mission or after the mission is over when the grateful amazement of having survived the mission settles in.

I saw Byron in the office the next day. We had an honest discussion of the physiology of what had happened, but the unexplained part was that it was unclear what triggered this hyperventilation in the first place. Then he told me a story that I heard several times in the Air Force.

He had just returned from Christmas leave where he had enjoyed time with his wife and three children. But during this time off, his wife told him she was sick and tired of his numerous deployments and wanted him to get out of the Air Force and fly commercially. He told me that when he was in Vietnam, the strain of imagining the dreaded visit at the door by the chaplain telling her that her husband had been killed was incredibly hard for her. Many of her friends had lost their fighter-pilot husbands to combat. When he came home alive, she was thrilled. Now that he was flying in Iceland where the flying weather was terrible, all those fears had recurred. Over the years, several videos of F-4s crashing while trying to land had terrified her.

She told him that if he did not get out of the Air Force, she would divorce him and that their three children had reluctantly agreed with that plan.

Byron admitted that as he lined up his approach to land his F-4 the day before, his wife's threat came barging into his consciousness. Agitated by the memory of the fear and anger in his wife's words, he started to hyperventilate.

Unfortunately, then I made a serious mistake in my interview. I asked him if it was time for him to leave the Air Force. I should not have been so direct. I should have asked him a less threatening question first. This might have allowed him to develop his own logic pathway towards a conclusion he could accept. After a few moments of silence, he glared at me, tightened his fists and flew into a rage. After aggressively denouncing the "candy ass" medical profession, he stomped out.

This response has stayed with me forever. As I was to see countless times in the ER over the years, when women are anxious or frightened, they will commonly cry. A certain subset of men, however, when confronted with a heart-wrenching situation in the ER, may be silent for a few moments and then burst into a rage. After such an explosion, they will storm out the door. Often, I have been told, such patients can be found in the ER parking lot weeping their hearts out.

Colonel Brock sent Byron home on leave. He did not return to Keflavik and I lost track of him. However, my success in talking Byron out of ejecting from the F-4 made me a hero in the squadron.

Byron's reaction to our conversation did not alter my fine impression of Air Force officers and enlisted staff. Life in the military can impose terrific strains on family harmony. Byron was flying a high performance, dangerous aircraft, which was loaded on take-off with mostly explosive ammunition and jet fuel.

Multiple deployments that last for months away from the wife and children often imply that the family learns to get along fine without dad. When the father returns, there is an awkward dynamic containing a hidden question: "Dad, now that you are back, what is your role in the family? We got along just fine while you were gone." To make matters worse, a return from deployment is usually followed by more family separation so dad can go away for further training. It is little wonder that maintaining the "glue" of family togetherness requires desire, commitment and lots of heart.

I would have been delighted to have as my next-door neighbor practically anyone who had served in the Air Force. I found them to be intelligent, well educated, dedicated to the highest standards of honor, honesty, loyalty and fairness and invariably possessed with a good sense of humor. They stand out to me as among the finest group of men and women that I have ever had the pleasure to work with.

Emergency at Sea

The bright sunlight and warm temperatures of the Icelandic summer receded as the darkness, fog, rain and falling temperatures of October 1975 approached. And the wind! On some days, the wind was blowing so hard that in order to turn my VW Bug, I had to drive behind a building, make my turn and then come out the other side. My wife had spent the summer with me while she studied medicine in the Navy Clinic. Sadly, she had flown home the previous day to start her third year of medical school. My staff of sergeants could tell I was glum and so they treaded lightly.

I was seated in my office completing the paperwork on a young fellow who was leaving the service. A loud voice shattered the quiet followed by a bang on my door. A sergeant stuck his head in and said, "Hey doc, they need you on the flight line right now. The chopper crew is getting ready to launch for an over water rescue and they want you aboard NOW." I quickly stood up and dashed for the door. Fortunately, my emergency rescue box was already in my car. Once again, my dilapidated VW Bug was up to the challenge and roared to life.

As I approached the flight line, I could see that the giant Air Force rescue helicopter already had its props turning. I sprinted to the helicopter, losing my hat from the downdraft. The crew chief reached down, grabbed my forearm and lifted—no, swung—me into the helicopter.

The helicopter was the gigantic "Sea Stallion." Capable of lifting loads of over five tons, it was, at the time, the Air Force's most valued cargo helicopter. The flight engineer, Fred Michaelson, and I had met a few weeks earlier when I performed his annual flight physical examination. The flight medic was Todd Nelson. I had spent many hours the previous summer working with Todd to get his annual re-certification as a flight medic. With a cheerful smile, Fred handed me a set of headphones with a microphone so I could talk and listen to the crew. The pilot, Bob Johnson (real name), deserved his reputation as the best pilot in the squadron thanks to two grueling deployments during the Vietnam War.

I quickly glanced around at the other crew members. They were all wearing the required rubber anti-immersion suits. These suits, called "poopy suits", were designed to keep a crew member who ditches into the ocean warm enough for a rescue team time to fish him out of the 32-degree water of the Atlantic---before he dies of hypothermia. However, because this was a hurry-up emergency launch, I had had no time to recover my poopy suit from the Phantom hangar---when it should have always been in my car! There I sat in my cotton and polyester clinic uniform. I thought to myself, "No Chris, you are not yet organized enough to be an ER doc."

I could hear the tower over the radio saying, "Rescue 14. You are cleared for takeoff. Southwest wind 15 knots gusting to 25. Switch to frequency...." I could not hear the rest of the radio frequency assignment as the roar of the helicopter's huge engines drowned out all other sounds. Taking off directly into the wind, this huge mechanical beast rocked, rattled and rolled as the wind gusts battered it. After lift-off, the pilots turned the helicopter slightly to the left and headed out over the North Atlantic.

I joined Fred and Todd in the back of the belly of the helicopter. Along the left side of the aircraft was a long, metal basket in the shape of a stretcher. On the right side of the aircraft was a huge sliding door for entering and exiting the aircraft.

Fred's warm "welcome aboard" to me was interrupted by the pilot speaking over the intercom. "Hey, doc. Thanks for coming on such short notice. Here is the situation. We are heading toward a seventy-foot fishing trawler about forty miles out. The captain says that the sea conditions are "dog shit." The waves are about ten to fifteen feet, winds 20 knots (24 mph) and the ship is rolling some thirty degrees. When the ship rolled, one of the crew members was struck in the head by a block-and-tackle. The captain reports that he is unconscious and bleeding from his head wound."

As they listened to the pilot's report, the look that passed between Todd and Fred told me everything I needed to know about the danger and difficulty of this rescue effort.

The helicopter arrived over the ship thirty minutes later, flying along the left side of the trawler at about one hundred feet. The ship looked new. The booms on the multiple tall masts were systematically positioned over the forward and aft portions of the ship. The booms on the masts were designed to rotate so that they could lower and hoist nets from multiple angles. The ship was rocking, rolling, rising up over huge waves and crashing down the other side. The vertical masts were the real threat, as a mast, being raised into the air by a huge wave, could easily strike the rotating prop on the top of the helicopter.

Helicopter rescue medics enjoy special respect in the Air Force; they are all paramedics with the physical conditioning of paratroopers. As preparation for his descent from the helicopter, Todd was wearing a four-point harness around his chest. Fred connected a large hook to the ring attached to the harness. The hook was connected to a steel cable attached to a huge electric winch near the door. This cable would enable the medic to be lowered to the trawler. Once on the deck, he would place the patient in the basket to be hoisted back up to the helicopter. When the patient was safely on board, the hoist cable would be lowered back down and the medic would be lifted back up.

When Fred opened the large cargo door, cold air blasted inside with such force that we all had to grab onto something firm. Both men manhandled the basket to within a foot or two of the open door. For a few minutes, nothing happened except for the rocking and thumping of the bouncing helicopter.

I asked what was going on. Fred replied, "This is a common problem with overwater rescues in bad weather. Bob is asking the captain to steer the ship into the wind making it easier to keep the helicopter properly aligned for the medic drop. But the captain, I'm sure, is complaining that whenever he tries to go into the wind, the enormous waves push the bow right and left. That causes the ship to corkscrew through the water making the pick-up," he paused for a second, "almost impossible."

As I looked down on the deck, I could see two crewmen holding the injured seaman supine on a pad. Those crewmen did their best to keep the injured seaman from sliding on the wet deck with the roll and pitch of the ship. Everyone else was holding on to something immobile to keep from getting tossed around the deck. The patient was covered with a blanket with a wrap around his head. I saw blood on the deck and noted that the seaman was perfectly still.

I heard the pilot, ask through the intercom, "Hey, Todd, what do you think?"

After a pause, Todd responded, "Let's give it a go, sir. There is only one person to pick up and the ship isn't sinking or on fire." This was going to be all about Bob's flying skill and Todd's strength and courage.

Todd's best chance would be if the helicopter could drop to as low a height as safety permitted. The risk was huge. The monster main rotor blade swept through an arc of seventy-eight feet, which placed it turning directly above of the ship's masts. Even the slightest bump of a rotor blade against such a mast would send the helicopter crashing down either into the ocean or on top of the ship.

Understanding the danger, the Icelandic crew had unbolted the mast posing the greatest threat and lowered it onto the deck, facing aft, away from the patient. That helped. Todd gripped his hoist line and waited for the signal from Fred to jump. Bob was trying to stay aligned with the rolling ship, keeping the helicopter rotors above the masts in order to get Todd on to the deck quickly before the wind sent Todd soaring like a kite. Fred knelt at the open door, where he had a better view of where Todd needed to land than did the pilot. Due to the howling wind, Fred had to yell into the intercom to Bob, "A little right, back about five feet, careful, she has rotated ten degrees to port." When he saw the perfect opportunity, Fred pushed Todd out the door and, using the electric winch, he quickly lowered Todd to the trawler's steel deck. Although he landed hard, Todd immediately gave Fred a thumbs-up to assure him that he was unhurt.

Fred pushed the basket out the door and started to lower it. When he could see that the rotation of the helicopter was aligned with the movement of the deck, he allowed the basket lanyard to briskly lower the basket towards the deck.

Suddenly, a gust of wind pushed the basket forward and to the left side of the ship. The line connecting the helicopter to the basket became wrapped around one of the masts. With the helicopter on a leash to the ship, the pilot needed to have the helicopter dance with the ship, so both were moving together like they were waltzing. Fred eased out the hoist cable to put more slack in the line. If the pilot did not get it right and there was a sudden jerk on the line, it could destabilize the helicopter and cause a crash, killing the helicopter crew and probably sinking the ship in a fire ball of exploding helicopter fuel. Or if the crew chief disconnected the helicopter line, a dying man and rescue tech would be left stranded.

Todd moved toward the tangled cable and, with the speed of a frightened bear cub scaling a tree, he climbed the mast to reach the basket. Once he reached it, he had to hold himself aloft with his left hand and untangle the basket with his right above a pitching deck with the downdraft of a huge helicopter over his head.

Bob sitting in the right-hand pilot's seat did not dare look down to assess Todd's progress. He was fixated on keeping the ship and the helicopter waltzing together while Fred gave him progress reports on Todd's efforts. With amazing strength, skill and a surge of adrenaline, Todd unwound the basket from the mast. Fred gave Todd extra slack in the hoist cable so that he could slide down the mast and still hold on to the basket. When Todd reached the deck, he crawled across the pitching deck to reach the patient dragging the basket with him. Fred tightened the hoist cable slightly to keep the line from getting entangled again.

Once he reached the seaman, Todd reinforced the head dressing, strapped the patient into the basket, and placed blocks on both sides of his head to prevent rotation of his neck while the basket was being hoisted to the helicopter. Todd signaled Fred with a thumbs-up. Fred hoisted the patient to the helicopter door as fast as the winch would go. Fred, secured to the helicopter with a harness to keep him from falling out, reached out for the basket and pulled it inside.

Fred moved the patient toward me and rotated the basket so that I was at the head of the stretcher and able to take care of the wound. He then went back to the open door and retrieved Todd. I did a quick screening neurological exam on the seaman and was relieved to see him move his arms and legs when he reached to grab a blanket. He was not brain dead. After donning sterile gloves, I carefully opened the makeshift dressing that had been applied by Todd and the trawler's crew. The wound was terrible. He had been struck on the right side of his head just above and behind the ear lobe. Amidst the tangle of blood-matted hair, I was uncertain exactly what the wound looked like. But then he spontaneously rolled to his left, which further loosened the thin dressing still in place. Now I could see a jagged piece of fractured skull protruding out like the side view mirror of a car. I used my flashlight to examine the wound more closely. I thought that I saw brain tissue slightly bulging out from behind the open fracture. Rather than wrapping the wound, I simply held soft gauze at the side of the fracture and hoped for the best. My big concern was a possible neck fracture or that the patient could have a seizure or vomit and aspirate.

"Bob?" I called in the intercom. "This fellow has an open skull fracture with what might be brain tissue coming out of the wound. Not sure. He needs to go to the OR immediately."

Bob replied, "Roger that."

He pushed the throttles forward all the way and the monster engines roared. It was sixty miles from the trawler position to the helipad at the Reykjavik hospital. Riding a tailwind, Bob achieved a speed of 200 mph. We landed in Reykjavik in about twenty minutes. The Icelandic paramedics were waiting for us at the hospital's landing pad. At first, I wanted the seaman to be kept in the basket until they reached the hospital. However, the chief paramedic overruled me. To his credit, his team did a marvelous job of moving the patient to the stretcher while keeping his neck immobile and safeguarding the wound.

The next day, the story of our rescue was splashed all over the front page of the Icelandic newspapers. Incredibly, the patient had survived surgery and was in the ICU in Reykjavik. Several weeks later, I spoke to the neurosurgeon who reported that the seaman's recovery had been miraculous. He had lost some motor skills on his left side and had a speech problem. But amazingly, his memory and intellect seemed to have survived with minimal deficits.

The Icelandic government gave us an award ceremony and profuse thanks. I couldn't attend, as I was home on leave.

Reflecting back on this rescue years later, two features stand out to me. First, my life and that of the entire helicopter crew was in the hands of the pilot, Bob. Those hands on the controls in a buffeted helicopter combined with his years of experience required a skill set that we typically associate with top surgeons. *But even surgeons are not in danger of having the whole operating room team killed if they make a mistake.* Secondly, because Bob had immense confidence in Todd, the final decision to attempt such a dangerous rescue was actually made by Todd. Where does a young fellow get that kind of courage? He was willing to rescue a stranger at the risk of his own life. He could have enjoyed being a paramedic anywhere, but he chose the riskiest of assignments. These two talented men demonstrated for me just how diverse the term "first responder" can be.

Two weeks before my discharge in June 1976, I was invited to attend the Air Force's Association of Flight Surgeons conference in Florida. There, out of perhaps a hundred or more Air Force flight surgeons, I was awarded Flight Surgeon of the Year. In retrospect, I have always thought that preventing the F-4 crash was the reason.

My Air Force service ended on a humorous note. One afternoon two weeks after my discharge, I received the following call: "Captain Davis, I'm calling from Air Defense Command here in Colorado. I have good news and bad news. The good news is that you have been awarded the Air Force meritorious service medal. Congratulations! This is a most distinguished achievement! The bad news is that I have just checked with the warehouse and they tell me that they are fresh out of medals."

Becoming an ER Doc

Residency

In June 1976, I separated from the Air Force and was keenly looking forward to starting my Hopkins emergency medicine residency. The Johns Hopkins Hospital enjoys worldwide renown for excellence. The historical traditions of the Medical Center include a long line of famous physicians and surgeons who have advanced the practice of medicine in the United States. In exchange for this excellent medical training, residents are required to work their butts off.

To my surprise, I discovered that the Hopkins Emergency Department in 1976 was dingy, worn and not well equipped. Stretchers were separated with only yellow curtains that offered no privacy and most of them did not have modern monitoring equipment on the wall above the head of the bed. Several stretchers were bolted to the floor, which meant patients had to be transferred to a wheeled gurney in order to go to x-ray or other tests.

Interpersonal communication between the new residents fascinated me. Those residents from top-tier schools like Harvard, Yale, Hopkins, Columbia and Penn carried themselves with relaxed self-assurance. However, other residents, newly arrived from second-tier schools, felt the need to immediately establish their clinical credentials. In order to show they were equally qualified, they would often make comments about obscure clinical syndromes that had little to do with the case at hand.

The ER was physically divided into a medical side and a surgical side. The medical side was always full of patients; many had complex problems.

Often, because the medical patients needed blood and urine tests or EKGs and x-rays, it took longer to adequately evaluate their problems. During the daytime, the surgical side was usually less busy. However, from 6 p.m. until 4 a.m., it was wild. Presenting cases were predominately abdominal pains, lacerations, fractures, stab wounds, bullet wounds, blunt trauma—all seasoned with one or more intoxicants: alcohol, cocaine, you name it.

In order to experience the diversity of medical cases that each of these sides offered, emergency medicine residents would rotate each month between the medical and surgical side. We enjoyed this exposure and the opportunity to get to know other healthcare professionals in both arenas. While the medical residents worked five twelve-hour shifts per week, the residents on the surgical side worked twenty-four hour shifts every other day. When I was there, after finishing a twenty-four-hour shift, we had to staff the surgical outpatient clinic for another four hours.

We were all chronically exhausted. As the motto at Hopkins stated: "The problem with working only every other night is that you miss half the good cases." One would expect that the exhausting workload would make everyone impatient and short-tempered. Fortunately, the residents shared a "foxhole camaraderie." We bonded over our shared plight of being overworked. One night in the surgical ICU, I was taking care of several very sick patients, all of whom had had heart surgery earlier that day. By actual count, that night I used the paddles ten times to electrically shock patients' hearts that had developed dangerous rhythms. The next day, I was completely exhausted. On rounds with the cardiac surgeons the next day, the night nurse had my back. She accompanied me because she knew I didn't remember much of what had happened. However, when I was asked a pointed question by one of the other surgeons, I flubbed the answer. The surgeon smiled, squeezed my shoulder and asked, "Dr. Davis, am I to understand that out of your dad's 500 million sperm, you were the fastest?"

Another night, that same surgeon was with me in the surgical ICU at 3 a.m. In a quiet moment, I asked him, "What was the most important course that you have ever taken?"

Without hesitation, he replied, "Art. Studying art helped me to understand what I was seeing." This has been a concept that I have heard multiple times in my career.

This keen insight from a brilliant, nationally renowned surgeon reminded me that Hopkins' medical training was indeed a privilege.

The volume of material that an ER doc has to know is vast. The best way to master new information is to teach it. And so, as a way of solidifying my knowledge, the idea of teaching emergency medicine in a university hospital appealed to me.

Also, at Hopkins, I had discovered that the internal medicine residents quickly became impatient with me if they felt that my knowledge of internal medicine was inadequate. It became apparent that if I was to have legitimacy as a professor of ER medicine, I needed to expand my knowledge of internal medicine. In order to become board-certified in both emergency medicine and internal medicine, I needed one more year of an internal medicine residency.

By all accounts, I felt that I had done a good job at Hopkins and was interested in staying for one more year to finish the internal medicine board requirements. The director of the Department of Internal Medicine called me into his office and told me that his medical residents thought highly of me and hoped that I would stay at Hopkins for my internal medicine residency. I was delighted. Who would have thought that Chris-who-barely-survived-MIT would be invited to the finest internal medicine residency in America?

That evening, I took my wife out to dinner to celebrate. She was an intern at the George Washington University Hospital at the time. She was exhausted and stressed. We had been separated for a year while I was in Iceland and another two years while I was trying to survive my residency at Hopkins. When I told her that I had been invited to stay at Hopkins for another year, she threw down her fork, wailed, "When are you ever going to come home?" and burst into tears. The waiters graciously stayed away from our table while the other patrons were enjoying this unfolding drama.

I returned the next day to speak once again with the Hopkins Director of Internal Medicine. He smiled at my story, picked up the phone and a few moments later was having a jovial chat with someone about my situation. He hung up, shook my hand and said, "Congratulations, Chris. They'll take you in the internal medicine residency at Georgetown."

I enjoyed my year at Georgetown immensely. I functioned as a second internal medicine resident, which was perfect for me. The pace was much less intense; there were lots of medical conferences that I had time to attend. Because of my time in the Air Force and at Hopkins, I was the most experienced of the second-year medical residents. Therefore, the Georgetown administration gave me the "squad" of a few interns who needed a motivational tune-up. I turned them around in short order and I had fun doing so.

A year after finishing at Georgetown, I returned as an Attending Physician at George Washington University Hospital; the hospital where I'd begun as an intern. But first, I'll tell you about my most memorable cases at John Hopkins.

Late for Work

One summer evening in August 1977, Baltimore was soaking in a hot, humid and windless sauna. While en route to my night shift in the Hopkins ER, I stopped at a Seven-Eleven store to get my essential 16-ounce black coffee. The Seven-Eleven in the late evening was a good forecaster as to what that night in the ER was going to be like. At the cash register, a line of ten young males were all purchasing the same item: cold beer. Immediately, I knew that the night would be brutal. The misery of Baltimore's steamy evenings often led to irritability, hard drinking and violence. Added to this mix was the already rampant poverty, drug abuse and unemployment endemic to the Hopkins greater neighborhood.

In spite of these negatives, for someone who wants to become a good emergency medicine physician, the advantage of training at Hopkins is that you are exposed to a constant flood of patients who are seriously sick or injured. What I had not realized before I joined the program was that the Hopkins ER residency was only about three years old and, at that time, only two full-time faculty members were assigned to teach all of twelve full-time ER residents in my cohort. Perhaps because the ER residency was a new addition to the time-honored history and tradition of Hopkins, faculty and the residents from other departments looked down upon the ER residents. Their view was that ER physicians were only GPs who wanted guaranteed time off. Fortunately, my three years in the Air Force had given me excellent exposure to primary care medicine and I felt more confident than those coming to the ER residency right out of medical school.

The ER nurses were superb. They worked incredibly hard keeping up with the tidal wave of patients. However, it was often the residents who drove the nurses crazy. Charlene, one of the night shift charge nurses, gave me the scoop.

"The nurses here have been doing this for years. Some of the new residents from fancy Ivy League medical schools show up with no experience and start bossing us around. These newbie brats think they shit ice cream." When you have pissed off the nurses, you were in deep trouble.

On this particular evening, I was working on the "surgical side." I was pleased to learn that the other doc working with me that night was a surgical resident named Randy Evans. Randy was from Texas and well-liked. About six foot four, Randy's shoulders bulged out from under his scrubs as silent testimony to his years of playing football in Texas. Randy was raised on a farm, so he was accustomed to starting to work at 4:30 a.m. and not being done until the late evening. When I served in the Air Force, I was amused by the typical braggadocio so often found in Texans, but I found them to be hard workers and fine associates.

Surprisingly, Randy arrived in the ER in a foul mood. I asked, "Randy, what's with the pissy mood? Not enough coffee?"

"Oh Christ, tonight you and I have to work with Frank Tooley. One of the surgical chiefs rotated my ER assignment and so I ended up on this shit schedule."

I understood his anger. Dr. Frank Tooley was one of the senior residents in the general surgical program. Unfortunately, Frank had garnered a terrible reputation among the more junior surgical residents who had worked with him. He was viewed as bossy, critical, condescending and impossible to please. Acting like a grizzly bear with a sore paw, Randy growled, "Last week, my team took a bleeding aneurysm with a crashing blood pressure to the OR. Frank chewed my ass off because I hadn't done a rectal exam! I mean for God's sake; the patient was within seconds of dying and Frank kicks my butt for not doing the rectal."

I laughed. The surgical residents and I had developed a special relationship. I had agreed to take call on a schedule that matched Frank's. That made me a huge hero among the surgical residents; my presence meant they would not have to put up with his endless fault-finding. I was willing to work with Frank because I had a better understanding of what was causing his critical behavior. Again, my years in the Air Force had taught me much about the male ego. Often, the reason that surgical chiefs in a teaching hospital are insufferably critical is that they are nervous that their team of junior surgical residents will fuck up a case. Frank wanted to do cardiac surgery after his general surgery residency was completed. Chronically nervous about not being selected for such a prestigious program, he believed that being a micromanaging tyrant who created fear in his staff was the pathway to developing a reputation for clinical perfection and improving his chances for selection into the cardiac surgery fellowship. For all of its fame as a teaching center, in the 1970s, Hopkins had not made progress on teaching how to be a good leader of a surgical team.

Frank and his "trauma team" of two residents had time on their hands; they stopped by the ER about 9 p.m. to see what was going on. I interrupted my examination of a patient with a nasty burn and turned to greet them.

Frank stood in front with his junior residents arrayed behind him like military cadets. Frank, using a body language suitable for dealing with an errant child, asked me, "Chris, what is the story with that lady with belly pain on stretcher 5?"

Nonplussed, I answered in short order, "She is a 47-year-old female with epigastric and right upper quadrant colicky discomfort. She is intermittently nauseated but without vomiting, fever or peritoneal signs. Belly films and urine OK." (This was an era when abdominal CAT scans and ultrasound were not yet available.) "I suspect cholecystitis but the work-up is still in progress."

"What did her rectal exam show?"

Frank always asks this question and I was ready. "No rectal tenderness, stool guaiac negative." In other words, there was no blood in her stool.

Frank moved closer to me and growled, "Goddam it, Chris, what do I want to know?"

With the respectful formality that I always use when a police officer is writing me a ticket, I responded, "You want to know if she needs to go the OR tonight or if she can be turfed to the medical guys for further work-up."

I had an understanding of Frank's enormous ego needs so I had a litany of polite responses to Frank's caustic and patronizing recommendations: "absolutely, definitely, as soon as possible, glad you reminded me, good point, I'll add that, great idea, we won't waste time." The surgical residents felt that my responses were obsequious. Perhaps. But I understood that each of his ideas had a worthwhile teaching point. Frank and I understood each other. He made me feel like a lion trainer in a circus. He would snarl, growl and show his huge teeth, but I was skilled with a wooden chair.

This particularly hot, humid night brought us an excess of casualties from the evening's gang warfare, drug use, alcohol intoxication and countless fights; and with each succeeding admission of "warriors," the tension in the ER increased. By 11:30 p.m., I was exhausted. Since the ER did not provide us with any food and none of us had the time to eat in the cafeteria, my only food had been the PB and J that I had gobbled at noon. Every stretcher in the department was occupied with an intoxicated patient with the usual menu of non-life-threatening stab wounds, long bone fractures or facial swelling associated with a blow from the butt end of a large handgun. One gunshot wound to the left chest had just gone to the OR, following the shotgun blast to the hip and groin.

Sometimes, the patients' stories made me grin. One patient with a crushed cheekbone assured me, "Hey, doc, my girlfriend got pissed at me for dating her girlfriend and she whacked me up the side of my face with my brand new .357 Magnum. She didn't mean me no harm." His blow was to his right cheek. Ninety per cent of people are right-handed; such an assailant would have hit the victim's left cheek. The BS about the girlfriend was intended to throw me off the track and discourage me from calling the police. He was admitted and his wound was surgically repaired by the ENT team. I'm sure that the ENT team relished this case; it was a great training opportunity and generally not experienced in a more suburban ER. My attitude toward this case reminded me of an aphorism that says: "Social workers believe everything their client tells them. Detectives don't believe anything their client tells them." I tended to think like someone in the middle of these two extremes.

Midnight arrived and I felt a glimmer of hope. There was a fourth-year Hopkins' medical student due to report to work in the ER starting at midnight. At least six patients with lacerations on stretchers were lined up along the hall like taxis at the airport awaiting riders. All drunk, they all needed to have their wounds cleaned up and sutured. I was looking forward to some help.

At 12:05 a.m., my medical student still had not arrived. I checked with the nurses and then checked with the "medical side" of the ER. No sign of the student. At 12:10 a.m., my medical student still had not arrived. Now I was pissed. As the minutes crawled past, I became truly furious. I howled to anyone who cared to listen, "Where is that goddam med student?" Propelled by the anger that accompanies stress and exhaustion, I stomped around the ER muttering to myself, "So, help me God, I am going to the medical school dean first thing in the morning to make sure this worthless SOB gets taught a lesson about professional responsibility…"

Just then, the doors of the ER flew open and there stood a hospital security guard holding a silent, limp body in his arms. The security guard cried out, "This poor kid was just shot in front of the hospital! I found him on the steps."

A torrent of bright red blood was pouring out his left anterior chest. I could see from across the room that the collapsed victim was wearing a short white coat and a medical school name tag. Clearly, the patient was my overdue med student! I hollered, "Gunshot wound to the trauma bay." The highly experienced nursing staff in the ER all coalesced to the patient's side in a matter of seconds, while the guard laid him down on the stretcher in the "trauma bay."

The patient lying on the stretcher was a slender male; he was minimally conscious with an obvious bullet hole in his left chest. In a matter of seconds, the staff had the patient nude, thus revealing a blast hole to the left of his heart. A nurse called out, "Pulse barely palpable. Systolic BP 40, heart rate 160." The nurses summoned the anesthesia resident and the surgical trauma team STAT to the ER.

Randy was unable to come help me, as he was tied up delivering a baby. Knowing that I was on my own, I did a quick total body exam and turned the patient onto his right side. There was no exit wound in his back. That was good news for me, as I now had only one chest wound draining blood to the outside. Chest wounds can cause a whole host of disasters, including collapsing the lung, lacerating one or more of the two huge blood vessels in the chest, (such as the aorta and the pulmonary arteries), damaging the heart or cutting the spinal cord in two. This list is just the beginning.

The nurses quickly put in two IVs to run a lightly salted solution called Ringer's Lactate at top speed to try to bring his systolic BP to a target of 90. They applied a high flow oxygen mask to his face. The anesthesia resident had heard the call over the loudspeaker and arrived quickly. He inserted an endotracheal tube into the patient's trachea, which enabled the patient to get adequate oxygen. Whenever the anesthesiologist would squeeze the bag to force oxygen into the patient's lungs and then ease the bag to allow the patient to exhale, blood spurted up the endotracheal tube.

Speaking loudly to the nurses, I ordered, "Please send off trauma bloods to the lab. Set up for a chest tube insertion and a central line." I quickly donned surgical gloves and painted the patient's left chest with Betadine to sterilize the skin. I grabbed the scalpel from the tray and made a five-centimeter incision along the top of the fifth rib. Using a curved clamp, I spread the tissue between the two ribs and then rotated the curved clamp facing downward and forcefully punched the clamp into the chest. I put my finger in the hole to make sure that no lung tissue was sticking to the inside of the rib cage. When I removed my finger from between the ribs, an enormous torrent of blood poured out through the hole. Using the curved clamp again, I locked the clamp around the edges of a chest tube and forced the tube into the chest between the ribs and the lung tissue. Blood gushed out of the chest into the chest tube and flowed out into the blood collection bag. No doubt about it; the patient had to go to the OR immediately.

"Roxanne, tell the blood bank we need six units of O pos blood super stat." To stay alive, this patient would need massive blood and fluid replacement. With a speed that in retrospect amazes me, I inserted a large IV catheter into the large vein under his left collar bone and we now had access to administer a large quantity of IV fluids.

Managing such a case is tricky. The patient needs to have his blood pressure raised to a systolic BP of 90. What is the point of giving clear fluids like Lactated Ringer's solution when the patient needs blood as fast as possible? When the blood pressure is very low, indicating a dangerously low blood flow, the blood vessels tend to collapse, restricting delivery of blood to the brain and coronary arteries. Unless corrected as soon as possible, the patient will die in a few minutes. To buy time, the Lactated Ringers will re-open the blood vessels with enough fluid to carry his meager inventory of blood to the brain and heart muscle to keep him alive.

Monitoring the blood pressure in a penetrating wound to the lungs is crucial. While the blood vessels open up, if you are lucky, platelets will plug the holes in the lung's blood vessels. However, if you raise the systolic blood pressure too high, the rising BP can blow out the delicate clots that are trying to stop the bleeding. Then the bleeding restarts in force.

By the time I'd administered the IV fluids, Frank and the rest of the OR team had arrived. Portable x-ray showed a collapse of the left lung with a big lake of blood floating in the chest cavity. I did an instant survey of what we had accomplished so far: CBC, chemistries, ordered four units of O+ packed red blood cells with a type and cross for more blood if needed, EKG and more. Foley catheter in the bladder? Check. Oxygen level via ET tube with 100% oxygen? Arterial oxygenation adequate.

Another nurse called out, "OR is ready. Let's go."

As the patient was being wheeled out of the ER, it suddenly occurred to me that the rest of Frank's OR team had done damn little to help me out. I was irritated, but too "amped up" to dwell on it.

Frank and his team left to go scrub in the OR. Before he left, Frank turned to the surgical residents on the OR team and remarked, "OK gentlemen, that is how a trauma code should be run. Chris has just demonstrated the finest trauma resuscitation I have ever seen."

Two surgical residents, two nurses and the anesthesia resident whisked the patient through the double doors and dashed to the elevator to go to the

OR. I was still breathing hard when I crashed down into a chair. Two of the nurses came up and rubbed my back. "Fabulous Dr. D. You did good!"

What Frank wanted to demonstrate to the other surgical residents was what a well trained and experienced ER doc could do by himself in a desperate situation. Frank identified me as the standard for clinical excellence. The surgeon with the highest standard for perfection used me to demonstrate what such perfection looked like. Wow!

I took a deep breath and got back to work. Then, oh my God, I looked down the hall. Where there had been six lacerations awaiting suturing before, now there were eight! Fortunately, all of the lacerations were superficial with no detectable damage to blood vessels, nerves or tendons. I sent two to x-ray to rule out subtle fractures or retained foreign bodies. After I had injected local anesthesia into the edges of each wound, the nurses scrubbed each of the lacerations with antiseptic solution and rinsed them with sterile saline. Feeling like John Wayne in an old Western, I grabbed the stapling gun designed for closing superficial wounds and charged down the line repeatedly squeezing the handle. Clank! Clank! Clank! Not beautiful closures but certainly sufficient. Next, nurses bandaged up the wounds. I finished their charts and gave them all referrals to the surgical clinic for staple removal in ten days. The two who went to the x-ray room just needed wound cleaning and closure like the rest.

Through the grapevine, I heard many months later that the medical student had survived and graduated from the Hopkins School of Medicine with the rest of his class. Reportedly, he was an insulin-dependent diabetic who had gone into a local convenience store to get something to eat during the long night shift ahead. The attackers followed him to the hospital where they shot him and stole five dollars off him. His parents sent me a wonderful thank-you note, which I cherished for many years.

Understandably, but to my irritation, the dean did not require him to return to the ER to complete his rotation.

Testing Faith

Shortly after midnight in the spring of 1978, while working on the medical side of the ER, I heard the rescue squad radio crackle:

"Hopkins, this is Medic 5. We are en route with a 16-year-old female with a reported overdose from a sleeping medication. She is somnolent but breathing well. BP 110/60; pulse 68, RR 12, pulse ox of 96. (normal vital signs). She responds to pain, but speech is garbled. We picked her up at a friend's house, so parents are not with us. There in three minutes."

The Hopkins ER had a special room that was used to treat overdoses. Fortunately, this room was well equipped with a monitor, IV, oxygen, suction and a sheet-covered stretcher. But this stretcher had four-point restraints. Patients who have overdosed on certain medications such as amphetamines can be violent; they may try to assault ER staff. This room was designed to handle these patients and the ER staff safely. Surrounded by solid, rather than curtained walls and painted battleship gray, it looked like a gloomy cell. It also had two solid doors. This ensured that if a patient became dangerous and slammed a doctor or nurse against one of the doors, a rescue team could quickly enter the other door.

A few minutes after their radio call, the paramedics rolled into the ER and took their stretcher straight to the OD room. I immediately joined them at the patient's side. She appeared to be of Nordic heritage; she was a slender, blue-eyed blonde with a ponytail—the cheerleader type. She was somnolent and slowly responsive to verbal stimuli. Fortunately, her vital signs were the same as those the paramedics had reported. Assured that she was stable for the moment, I stepped outside the room to speak with Tom McCoy, the paramedic, while the nurses got the routine steps underway.

"Dr. Davis, we received a call about thirty minutes ago about a teenage girl who had taken an overdose. The patient was not at her home but at the home of a girlfriend. The patient's friend is a 16-year-old girl named Julie who attends the same high school as the patient. She told us that the patient's name is Linda Antenola and that Linda had taken an overdose of over-the-counter sleeping pills." Tom reported that Julie went on to explain how the overdose had happened. Around 10 that evening, Linda had come running over to Julie's house sobbing and totally distraught. Julie had brought her into her bedroom and closed the door so that her parents would not hear anything. Linda revealed that her father, who is a devout religious fundamentalist, had discovered that she was sleeping with her boyfriend and that night he had erupted into a rage and threatened her with multiple ways the Lord was going to punish her.

After telling Julie about this angry encounter with her father, Linda confessed to Julie that the situation at home was so terrible that she had already taken a handful of sleeping pills. Having admitted this, Linda abruptly got up, stormed into Julie's bathroom and locked the door. Frantic because she could not get Linda to open the door, Julie found a pin to put into the door handle to unlock it. She rushed in and found Linda sitting dazed and barely talking. Julie called 911 and continually tried to call Linda's parents multiple times but the line was always busy.

After Tom had summarized all of these details, I asked him, "Tom, was Julie able to tell you what she had taken?" Tom then reached into his pocket and handed me a pill bottle. It was labeled Benadryl, a well-known over-the-counter sleep aid whose generic name is diphenhydramine. The label listed 100 tablets and was empty but obviously I had no idea when or how many tablets she had taken.

Tom and I quickly returned to Linda in the OD room. The nurses, Sheila and Barbara, had applied oxygen, started an IV and had sent bloods off to the lab. Charlie, our ER tech, was assembling much of the gear that we would need. This gear is stored outside the room so that patients cannot have access to its contents, which include medications and syringes.

Tom looked over at me, his face revealing deep concern and asked, "Dr. Davis, what is the toxicity of diphenhydramine?"

"Unfortunately, Tom, diphenhydramine overdose is very tough to handle. The medication in large doses can cause virtually every possible nasty effect. These include seizures, rapid heart rate, slow heart rate, respiratory arrest and damage to the heart's ability to generate the electrical signal needed to keep the heart beating."

Turning to Linda, I gave her a quick, focused examination. Her head, lungs, heart, abdomen and extremities showed nothing unusual: no needle tracks or bruises. Next, I pressed my knuckle hard against her breastbone. This maneuver is quite painful but helps to determine how sedated a patient is. She only made a weak attempt to brush my hand away. However, in a matter of minutes, her BP was down to 90/60, her pulse had dropped to 64, her pulses were feeling weaker and her pupils were dilated. I became immediately worried. She was going downhill fast.

"Sheila, would you please call Poison Control for me?"

While Sheila was making the call, I ordered an EKG for Linda. The electrocardiogram is basically a meter that measures the amount of voltage in various parts of the heart along with the electrical pattern of the heart muscle contractions and provides a paper readout. Barbara, the other nurse helping me, handed me Linda's EKG. What should have been the tall, narrow signal, called the QRS, was in Linda's case, suspiciously short and wide.

In order for heart muscle to contract, it receives a small jolt of electricity. This jolt is made by tiny heart cells called the "pacemaker." In an EKG, the most prominent feature of the tracing is the "QRS complex." When the QRS is tall and skinny, that tells us the pacemaker cells are making enough voltage for the heart muscle. However, when the pacemaker cells become sick, the shape of the QRS changes; it becomes shorter and wider. This dangerous pattern was what I was starting to see in Linda's EKG, and it warned me that her heart was having trouble generating enough of an electrical signal to keep the heart muscle pumping blood. Unfortunately, diphenhydramine is famous for damaging pacemaker cells.

Overdose patients that are this deeply sedated require immediate support for their breathing. I put an endotracheal tube down Linda's windpipe and secured it with tape. Barbara continued to supply oxygen to the patient by squeezing the bag that forces air into the lungs. Sheila reported, "I've called the respiratory therapist, he's coming down with a ventilator."

Now that her airway and breathing were addressed, I decided to not lavage her stomach to wash out the pills because I suspected that the sixty-minute time limit for doing so apparently had already passed. Instead, the nurses and I threaded a large soft plastic tube into her stomach and pushed in activated charcoal into her stomach to absorb as much remaining portion of the diphenhydramine as possible that had not already entered her bloodstream. Activated charcoal is a ground-up mixture of coal and wood that has been heated to a very high temperature and has an "activating agent" added. This process turns the powder into a slurry with a high surface area. Think of it like a small sponge being converted into a large sponge. This huge surface area makes it easier for the activated charcoal to absorb the pills that have caused the poisoning.

"Dr. Davis, Poison Control is on the phone."

I picked up the phone and heard a courteous, crisp voice with a hint of a British accent. "Dr. Davis, this is Ian Clark from Poison Control. How can I help you?"

"Ian, thanks for calling. I have a 16-year-old diphenhydramine overdose. We have a witness, empty bottle of pills and a preceding emotional trauma. I don't think anything else is involved but the toxicology report won't be back for hours. I intubated her a few minutes ago and her oxygen level is looking better. The nurses are putting in the activated charcoal as we speak. However, her heart rate is slowing. I'm running half-normal saline with two amps of sodium bicarbonate wide open to keep her pressure above 100. I think she'll need IV epinephrine."

Epinephrine given intravenously is a powerful drug only used in the ER in desperate situations. Epinephrine has two properties: it increases the rate and force of contraction of the heart muscle and it tightens the arteries to raise the blood pressure. Epinephrine is administered through a large IV catheter to get to the heart quickly. Worried that her blood pressure was going to crash, I inserted such a large IV catheter into the large vein under her collar bone. That way, if she needed epinephrine, it would not be a long trip from the injection site to her heart.

"Do you have any idea how many tablets?"

"The label said 100 tablets, but the bottle was empty".

After a moment of silence, Ian asked, "What does her QRS complex look like?"

Barbara ran a short strip off the monitor so I could look at the QRS. I told Ian, "It's getting wider." I vaguely remembered some of the details of treating a diphenhydramine overdose. However, I was confronted by a teenage girl in the prime of her life who was starting to die. I was rattled.

Ian explained, "It appears that she is starting to suffer from slow sodium channel injury that is damaging her ability to generate the QRS signal."

"Got it. As I remember, we need to give IV sodium bicarbonate, lots of it. My nurse has already given her two amps of bicarbonate IV push in a peripheral line and one milligram of epinephrine IV push through the central line."

Ian then walked me through the details of how to manage such an unusual but life-threatening overdose. To be honest, I was so frightened by this impending tragedy that I could not think for myself. I needed Ian there to help. Given how upset I was becoming, I didn't trust my decision-making.

Barbara, without my asking, handed me another EKG strip. Whereas the first QRS on her initial EKG seemed a bit too short and too wide, this second QRS signal clearly demonstrated that the QRS was becoming shorter and wider; it resembled a rapidly melting snowman. The damage to the QRS was happening so fast!

Barbara checked the blood pressure with a manual cuff and reported, "BP 60/40. Very hard to hear the pulse with my stethoscope."

I felt her carotid artery in her neck with my fingertips. I could not feel a pulse.

I ordered, "Let's start CPR. Charlie, you pump. Sheila, please stand by to do meds. Barbara, please apply the external pacer and watch the QRS morphology." I turned to the newly arrived respiratory therapist, Jose Alvarez, and said, "Jose, forget the ventilator for now. Just continue bagging her." To "bag" a patient means to squeeze the bag connected to the endotracheal tube that sends oxygen down into the lungs.

Charlie, our tech, was a young fellow in his thirties who had earned a GED. He loved pumping as it made him feel, correctly, that he had the most important job at the moment. Only about five-foot-four, he grabbed a stool, stood on it, leaned over the patient and started cardio-pulmonary resuscitation at 100 pumps a minute. I knew that he worked out in the gym a lot and had some confidence in his ability to pump on Linda's chest as long as needed. Unfortunately, it was now clear that Linda's heart had lost its interest in beating.

I palpated the carotid pulse in her neck and felt reassured by the positive beat in her neck that I could feel with every one of Charlie's compressions. But then, after a minute or two, I had Charlie pause. I could no longer feel a pulse. I asked Charlie to restart the compressions and asked Sheila to call Ian back.

"Dr. Davis, Ian's on the line."

"Ian, this is Chris. We've lost a pulse. We have now been doing CPR for fifteen minutes and are giving her the IV dose of one milligram of epi every few minutes."

"What does the QRS look like?"

"Barbara, please give me a short rhythm strip."

We stopped CPR for a few seconds while Barbara ran the QRS strip and handed it to me. Charlie promptly resumed CPR.

"Ian, looks like a sine wave with almost no height." At this point, we had been doing CPR for about twenty minutes and had given her another two ampules of sodium bicarbonate. Charlie continued to do CPR while Ian and I discussed possible options that really had no likelihood of making any difference. I asked Charlie to quit pumping again. We all looked at the cardiac monitor on the wall. On the screen, we could see the image of the QRS becoming wider, then wider. I told Charlie to resume the pumping. Two minutes later, I told him to stop. We all looked at the monitor: flat line. Our QRS showed a few weak wavy lines for two or three seconds and then again…flat line. I could not feel a pulse. Linda was gone.

Barbara and I stared at the QRS flat line. Barbara's eyes welled up with tears while I felt overwhelmed by the silent testimony of the lump in my throat. Sheila left the room sobbing. Charlie gave Barbara a warm, long hug.

I spoke to Ian and said: "We have lost her. I just declared her. Ian, thanks for your help…but…but I have to go now." I thanked Ian using that soft voice that we all know signals impending tears and quietly hung up.

Linda's parents didn't know. Linda died alone.

I was grateful to Ian. As a poison control expert, he walked my stressed brain through the correct procedures to care for Linda. Even though she died, Ian's help that night relieved me for the rest of my life of subsequent worry that I might not have done everything right.

About an hour after I had declared Linda dead, I was standing in the hallway talking to a resident. A stretcher, covered with a white sheet, rolled by me. It was Linda on her way to the morgue. In a matter of minutes, my heartbreak turned from grief to a deep anger for this avoidable death that I still feel forty years later.

Linda didn't want to die. She went to her friend's house assuming that she would be rescued in time by her friend. With frontal lobes of the brain not fully matured, teenagers frequently experience sudden mood swings and act impulsively without being fully aware of the consequences. This is especially difficult when the crisis challenges rigid parental values. Supporting a teenager calmly through such an emotional trauma is possibly the biggest challenge parents can face.

The Worst Sore Throat Ever

The case that I dreaded the most but that ER docs rarely encounter presented at Hopkins on my shift one evening in late November in 1977. I was working on the surgical side of the ER when a nurse rushed in and said, "Dr. Davis, it's urgent; they need you on the medical side."

Fortunately, the surgical side of the ER at that time was actually stable. Nobody on the surgical side was "crashing" thanks largely to the weather. ER work was, to a large degree, related to the seasons. The hot summer months in Baltimore, as I described in an earlier case, were the busiest time for the surgical side. Young people were out playing sports, partying and drinking. Alpha males often ended up in fights, arms got broken sliding into home plate and sailors got bonked on the head by the boom of their sailboats and so on. But by late autumn in Baltimore, the ER situation had changed. Temperatures hovered in the 40s and brisk winds often blew. Diseases like pneumonia and flu had begun to take on a bigger role. On this particular night, the medical side was busier than the surgical side.

Responding to the nurse's call for help, I hurried across the hall to the medical side where I encountered two very scared residents. One of them was medical, the other was in anesthesia. They were hovering over the head of a patient who was sitting up on the stretcher, gasping for air and turning blue. When the skin starts to turn blue, the problem is almost always hypoxia— lack of oxygen. The patient was huge. He was a Baltimore longshoreman and had been doing heavy lifting all of his life. Short, wide and very muscular, he was the perfect body type to play nose tackle in the NFL. He also had the shortest neck you could imagine.

The medical resident reported, "Chris, we are in trouble here. This patient came in about twenty minutes ago with a fever and difficulty breathing. He was clutching his throat and I thought that he was choking on a piece of food. He couldn't talk, would not lie down and had stridor." The resident was describing a high-pitched sound that a patient, whose upper airway is partially blocked, makes when he tries to inhale. Sitting up makes it slightly easier to breathe.

In a loud panicky voice, the anesthesia resident added, "This guy has a huge epiglottis. It is swollen, cherry red and so enlarged that I cannot get the endotracheal tube in."

The anesthesia resident was clearly in a bind. Ideally, the patient would be taken to the OR, sedated and the endotracheal tube would be inserted into the lungs using a fiber optic scope. Now, there was no time.

"The IV is in," reported one of the nurses. Now at least, some sedation could be delivered while we tried to fix this huge longshoreman's problem.

Epiglottitis! If I was going to save the patient from dying from hypoxia, I did not have a moment to lose. The trachea (windpipe) has a small protective trap door located at its top. That door flops down over the top of the trachea whenever we swallow. Without it, the food could very easily drop down into the trachea. The epiglottis is thin, flat and about as big around as your thumb but is much thinner. Unfortunately, the epiglottis can become infected.

As it becomes red and inflamed, it swells. This swelling makes the epiglottis immobile. Therefore, it cannot lift up when the patient is trying to breathe. So, this little flap covers over the trachea that it is designed to protect. Unable to breathe, the patient panics until he becomes so oxygen-deficient that he collapses. Death is moments away.

I moved closer to the patient's stretcher. He was wearing an oxygen mask. Despite the oxygen, the muscles over his ribs were moving in and out as he valiantly struggled to breathe. Using a bag-mask to help him was out of the question, as such positive outside pressure would simply push the epiglottis down over the trachea. I realized that there was only one thing I could do to save this man's life. Despite my high anxiety, I needed to immediately cut a hole into his windpipe and place a plastic tube into this hole, which would permit the air to bypass the epiglottis. This surgical procedure is called a cricothyroidotomy. The membrane that connects the thyroid cartilage (Adam's apple) to the cricoid cartilage in the anterior neck lies directly over the trachea. Cutting through this membrane provides quick access to the trachea. I turned to the nurse and barked, "Bring the tracheostomy tray stat from the surgical side and get me a surgical light." There was no time to say "please" or "would you mind?" In moments the tray appeared. I noticed that the tape used to secure the top of the kit was dry and curling at the edges. Clearly, it had not been opened recently.

I donned surgical gloves and wiped the patient's anterior neck with Betadine antiseptic. He was now lethargic, and his entire body was turning blue. The anesthesia resident held his head firmly while the nurse quickly positioned the portable OR light. I took a scalpel and made a vertical incision into the anterior neck below the larynx. The Adam's apple is located at the top of the larynx and is a valuable landmark. After opening the skin and spreading it apart, I next made a horizontal cut into the cricoid cartilage. Using a curved clamp, I spread the membrane apart and was relieved to hear air rush into the trachea. Next, I took the curved plastic tube and tried to insert it into the airway. The process felt like pushing a big button through a buttonhole that was too small. After one failed try, I was able to wiggle the tube into the trachea. This time, a much larger rush of air came out of the tube and reassured me that it was properly placed. The anesthesia resident immediately began putting air into the tube with his bag while I started to secure the tube. My heart was pounding like the drums in a rock band and my mouth was almost too dry to talk. The final step should have been easy: putting tape around the patient's neck to keep the tube from falling out.

"Oh Christ," I yelled, "He's waking up." At that moment, the patient promptly sat up while I was desperately trying to keep the plastic airway from falling out. Dazed and still oxygen-starved, the patient had no idea what was happening. I begged him, "Please sit, hold still. You are doing much better." I tried to push him back down so I could hold the tube while we tied it in place. Then, with the resolve of an enraged bull, he took his massive hands and wrapped them around my chest. With all of his newfound strength, this burly longshoreman catapulted me into the air like a misdirected football, causing me to crash to the floor. Oh God! As I struggled to my feet, my first thought was to run away before he killed me. But doing so would kill him. With lightning speed, the anesthesia resident gave him an ample dose of a sedative. In a few seconds, he slumped back onto the stretcher. A moment later, he coughed. Since his airway had not yet been tied down, his cough and his body movements dislodged his brand new, potentially life-saving airway and tossed it onto the floor!

He needed a replacement airway STAT. So now that my team and I were fully rehearsed, I slapped some more Betadine onto the wound, donned a fresh pair of surgical gloves and put in another airway. Thank God, the tray actually had two. I inserted the new tube and tied the tag lines around his neck. "Not too tight," the nurse warned.

Partway through this procedure, the head nurse called the Ear, Nose and Throat resident. Driving in from home, he arrived in about twenty minutes. He took the patient to the OR where he cleaned up the wound and sutured the tracheal airway in place. He was most complementary about how we handed the emergency. However, this being Hopkins, the case was forgotten almost immediately as more amazing, scary and challenging cases continued to pour through the door.

I learned from one of the nurses that he went to the ICU for antibiotics and wound care. He went home in five days. Adult cases of epiglottitis are rare, and I had never done a cricothyroidotomy on a living person before.

Emergency medicine physicians frequently stumble across a great paradox in their career development. They have a choice of either the high stress excitement and experience of an inner-city ER or the less stressful suburban/ rural ER that is more manageable over a long career. Training in an inner-city hospital ER gave me the opportunity to be in charge, make life-saving decisions on the spot and to do those fast, life-saving procedures that I felt were necessary. The Hopkins ethos being what it was in those days, the specialty residents were usually too overwhelmed with their own work to come to the ER to bail me out of trouble. I often felt crushed by the stress.

When I moved to a suburban hospital ER that had dozens of doctors on the medical staff, my decisions were more often made, and procedures performed in conjunction with specialists in the related areas. To my surprise, I missed my independence. I missed the action. But I recognized that burnout is highest in the urban ER. So, like many other ER docs, I eventually gravitated to hospital settings where the stress level was tolerable and where I felt I could work for a lifetime.

Teaching Emergency Medicine

An Attending Physician at a University Hospital

In eighth grade, I was having more difficulty learning algebra than I should have. One evening, my dad told me, "The best way to learn a complex subject is to teach it." For two or three weeks thereafter, my dad would sit down with me in the evening and we would study an algebra problem that he had dreamed up. Playing the role of a stumped student, he would say, "I don't understand this problem. Can you help me with it?" When I started to explain the very first problem, he said, "Stop there. Here's the key. Don't show me how to solve the problem, teach me how to solve it by asking me questions. *Remember, Chris, most of us don't remember the answer to the question that nobody ever asked us*" He taught me the short-cut version of the Socratic Method. I loved the process and my struggles with algebra ended when I knew it well enough to explain it.

My long-ago experience of learning algebra by teaching it may have been at the root of my decision during my residency training to pursue Emergency Medicine in a teaching hospital. After finishing my second residency program at Georgetown, I returned to George Washington University Hospital to work as an ER Attending Physician. By 1979, the GW ER was developing a well- trained corps of full-time emergency physicians. The challenges that so troubled me as an intern in 1972 had been mostly fixed.

The physician who has primary responsibility for a patient's care is called the "attending physician". The role of an attending physician in the ER of a teaching hospital has special challenges. First, he or she is responsible for ensuring that good quality care is provided to all patients. Toward this end the attending makes sure patients are expeditiously evaluated and mobilizes the proper teams for best care.

Secondly, the attendings must frequently prioritize the patient caseload. They decide which patient needs emergency care STAT and in what order the other patients should be seen. The attending makes recommendations and final decisions about patient care: Who goes home? Who goes to the ICU? Who goes to the medical floor? How best to manage the drunk with a broken ankle who wants to stagger out of the ER to get a drink? Part of overseeing patient care requires consultations with those residents who are providing patients with specialty care such as pediatrics or orthopedics. The attending makes sure that each patient's needs are identified and properly dealt with as soon as possible not only to provide quality care but to keep the flow of patients moving through the department.

Thirdly, the attending is a teacher and trains and supervises the often-large cadre of residents and medical students who are working with him or her in the ER. Each department in a university hospital has a hierarchy of instructors: professor, associate professor, assistant professor and instructor. Newly appointed professors starting in an academic hospital have the rank of assistant professor. They have finished their training. An attending physician in the ER is, at a minimum, an assistant professor and is the most senior professor on duty.

Finally, on behalf of the patients and the students, the attending ensures that professionalism and cordiality are always maintained and routinely jousts with administration over resources and policies.

Teaching emergency medicine to residents and medical students was the most enjoyable part of my career. My teaching method harkened back to my father's example. A resident might say, "Dr. Davis, the patient is having terrible back pain and has blood in his urine. It looks to me like a kidney stone."

Then I might reply, "He might indeed have a kidney stone. But our job is to rule out the most dangerous possibilities first. What else might he have?" Having heard from the resident a list of remote possibilities, I might say, "Could this be a ruptured aneurysm in his abdomen?" A burst of enlightenment would then flash across the resident's face and he would dash off to investigate that possibility.

Man, that was fun. I felt I made a valuable contribution to my students' education. Of course, sometimes the pressure of incoming patients did not allow time for such a didactic approach; when necessary, I made suggestions for the appropriate course of action. In addition to one-on-one instruction, I also developed and presented lectures for the students and residents. Best of all, I enjoyed opportunities to continue to learn new and sometimes controversial information at conferences and to interact with the rest of the medical staff.

Nevertheless, the job of being the attending physician in a busy university hospital was tough. Often, it felt to me like being a fire chief directing his team of firefighters to conquer a blaze that never stopped burning!

No wonder then that Emergency Medicine has the highest rate of "burnout" among practicing physicians. This is understandable given the amount of stress inherent in this role. I, however, thoroughly enjoyed all these challenges of being an ER attending physician; I was fortunate to be surrounded by many colleagues who felt the same. George Washington University Hospital fostered a warm atmosphere of friendship and cordiality and so I developed solid friendships during this time. The following two cases stand out from my years there as an attending physician.

Jade Napkin Ring

As I took a sip of my coffee and checked out the position board specifying the current patients, a tall, second-year medical resident named Phil approached me and said, "Doctor Davis, you are not going to believe this."

"Really? What have you got?"

Grinning broadly, he said, "Please let me show you. Follow me."

We both entered the patient's room where I saw a young male about twenty-five writhing in agony. Next to him stood a young woman in her twenties who was gently stroking his shoulder with tears pouring down her face. Phil introduced me to the patient named Jake and identified me as the "emergency department supervisor." I never liked being called a "supervisor" as it had a disciplinarian ring to it. I would have been more comfortable if he had introduced me as, "This is Dr. Davis. He is a professor of emergency medicine and is here to help us."

Phil gently pulled down the sheet covering Jake's genitals YIKES! Jake's penis was massively swollen and deep purple. At the base of his penis was a ceramic ring of some type. Just in front of this ring was the sort of combination padlock that we all used in our high school lockers.

"Jake, how did this happen?"

With frightened eyes, Jake said not a word but turned to his girlfriend.

His girlfriend blurted out, "Oh doctor, this is so awful. We were having sex. Afterward, I wanted Jake to know that I wanted him forever. And so, as a sign to assure me that he would always be mine, I slid this jade napkin ring over his—you know—. To make sure that it did not fall off, I put the padlock in front. We then fell asleep. At about 6, he woke complaining of terrible pain—down there."

"Oh, doc, you gotta help me. Am I going to lose my dick? The pain is killing me!"

I examined Jake and was immediately worried. His penis was the size of a large beer bottle and the color of a huge bruise. The big concern here was whether or not the jade napkin ring and the padlock had caused so much swelling as to choke off the arterial blood supply to his penis. I put on a pair of sterile gloves and gently pressed on the skin. It blanched very slightly telling me that there was still blood flowing into his penis but there was not another minute to lose.

"Phil, please put in an IV, give him something for pain while I talk to engineering." I then walked over to the nurses' station and asked the clerk to call maintenance for me right away.

A few minutes later, the clerk reported that maintenance was on the phone. I walked back to the nurses' station to answer this return call.

"Good morning, this is Dr. Davis. Are you the fellow in charge of maintenance today?"

"Yep" was the reply with what sounded like a crisp New York City accent. "My name is Noah. What's the problem?"

Doing my best to whisper so that the whole department would not be too interested in this problem, I explained, "We have an honest to God medical emergency here and I need your help. Would you please bring us a bolt cutter right away? We have a patient in deep trouble from a padlock." That did it. Every set of ears in the ER was now tuned in to follow this situation.

Within minutes, the maintenance engineer arrived and gave me a very skeptical look. I quietly whispered, "Noah, come with me. You will then understand." I was damn sure this was a violation of the patient's privacy. But I needed the maintenance engineer to see for himself how urgent the problem had become. A bolt cutter would make Machiavelli grin. With small black jaws and long red handles, it is designed to cut through steel—and looks like a torture tool.

After Noah had handed off the bolt cutter to me and left the room, I asked Phil, the resident, to hold the patient's phallus while I tried to get the ring of the padlock within the jaws of the bolt cutter. Unfortunately, the penis was so swollen that Phil had to apply lots of pressure to get the cutter's jaws around the padlock's metal ring. Once I felt confident, I squeezed the arms of the cutter. Snap! The metallic loop of the padlock was cut through. Unfortunately, the penis was so swollen that I was unable to rotate the metal loop of the padlock to get it off. Again, I cut the padlock from the other side. Snap! The cut loop of the padlock went flying off. Briefly airborne and then clanking on to the floor, the metal loop sounded like the empty cartridge flying out of a high-powered rifle. The force of this projectile attested to the amount of pressure the swollen penis was applying to the inside of the padlock loop.

"Jesus, doc! Is it still OK? Did you cut it? Have you ever done this before?"

While the small dose of morphine Jake had received had somewhat reduced his pain, his terror about the survival of his penis raged unabated.

"Relax, Jake. I do this all the time."

I applied gobs of lubricating gel around the penis and tried to gently rotate the napkin ring off. No go. His swelling was so severe that I could not even rotate the ring.

"Please get me the ring cutter."

So far, we were about twenty minutes into this struggle over penile entrapment when the mother of the girlfriend came charging into the room without knocking. As the mother and daughter tried to argue in a whisper, I told them both to leave. The painful sounds of hysterical sobbing came through the door. Their screaming expletives about "his dying pecker" ricocheted around the ER like bullets. By now both the staff and the patients were glued to the verbal firefight.

The ring cutter is a tiny, curve shaped saw with small teeth that is turned with a flat key suggestive of an old wind up alarm clock. I have never seen it fail on a ring, but this was different. I vaguely remembered from my engineering courses taken ages ago that jade is an amazingly hard gem.

Sliding the ring cutter's curved lower edge under the jade ring, I turned the handle. The little saw rotated valiantly but did not even leave a scratch. This was an affront to my manhood. After all, I had rowed crew in college and I still had a good supply of muscle left. I turned the handle as hard as I could. Again, the little saw flailed against the jade ring and just bounced off without leaving so much as a scratch. I tried harder. No luck.

"*Oh crap,*" I thought. Turning to Phil I said, "I bet that this ring cutter is too worn out. Please ask the nurse to get another.

Sharon, the charge nurse, came in and explained that this was the ED's only ring cutter. "In fact, Dr. Davis, the ring cutter is brand new. I just unwrapped it myself."

I knew that the OR crew was tied up with two cases. I would have loved to have sent him to the OR but calling in a third OR crew would have taken too much time. Time was getting critical. Quickly, I grabbed the phone.

"Noah? This is Doctor Davis again. I need help in a hurry. The bolt cutter got the padlock off, but our ring cutter just bounces off the jade. I need a ball peen hammer and an anvil STAT. The biggest Rambo-sized ball peen hammer you have and please hurry."

In a few minutes, I heard a clatter at the door as the trolley carrying an anvil and a BIG ball peen hammer were wheeled in. By this time, a nurse and an intern had also joined us to help.

"Jake, we've got to hurry. There are times in life to be brave and this is one of those times. The jade is too hard for the ring cutter. While jade is tough, I believe that tapping it with the rounded end of a ball peen hammer will shatter it."

By this time, Jake was shaking with terror. Again, he asked, "Doc, have you ever done this before?"

"Oh, lots of times. In fact, when a case like yours comes in, I'm the guy they call." My well-intended fib rewarded me with a blast of Irish Catholic guilt.

"So, doc, you're going to swing a hammer at my pecker? C'mon man!" Jake was probably thinking of an old Western movie where the huge blacksmith was using a massive hammer to pound horseshoes.

Squeezing his hand, I said "Jake, if I don't get this off, you'll never have another girlfriend again."

That did it. Jake was on board. "OK, doc, do what you've gotta do."

I had them stand Jake up by the side of the stretcher and hold him up in case he keeled over. I wheeled the dolly with the anvil as close to Jake as I could. His jade-embossed penis made a clunk as I laid it on top of the anvil. Holding the napkin ring between my two fingers, I gave the ring a gentle tap with the rounded end of the hammer. Clink. Nothing happened. Taking both a deep breath and with careful aim, I struck the ring with a more forceful blow. Clink. Nothing happened. Jake was a wreck. Soaked in sweat, trembling, his eyes were as big as saucers. I tried to think of alternatives. Maybe, if I placed a screwdriver over the ring and hit the screwdriver with the hammer it might... No, I thought, *what if the screwdriver went through the ring and stabbed his penis?*

I looked up to see the recently arrived nurse shaking all over; she quickly left the room. Then, taking careful aim, I raised the hammer to the height of my shoulder and dropped the hammer. Bang! The room was instantly blessed with the sound of tiny pieces of jade flying about striking the anvil, wall and floor.

Immediately afterward, Jake fainted. The resident and intern caught him and lifted him back onto the stretcher. He looked lifeless and Phil felt only a fast, thread-like pulse. He went quickly to the foot of the stretcher and lifted Jake's legs as high as he could. That brought a flood of blood from his legs to the rest of his body. Within seconds, Jake was coming around as his pulse and blood pressure returned to normal.

I examined Jake's penis and with gentle pressure saw a tiny blanch in the skin. The blood flow to Jake's organ was slowly being restored.

"Jake, I want you to promise me that from now on, you will be more careful with your gear. OK?"

At that moment, a nurse abruptly opened the door and said: "Doctor Davis, Carl needs you immediately. He's got a chest pain in room 2 that's crashing."

I gave Jake a friendly pat on the arm and dashed to room 2. As I left, I glanced at the clock and realized it wasn't even 9 a.m. yet.

Jake was admitted to the hospital by the medical residents with a urology consult. After much discussion, medical team started Jake on blood thinners to help dissolve the clots that undoubtedly had spread throughout this iconic symbol of manhood. He recovered well. Unfortunately, I heard later that the mother of his girlfriend went nuts with rage when she learned that I had destroyed the jade napkin ring.

When I reflect on Jake's potentially disastrous situation, I'm reminded of Bill Bryson's caution in his book, *The Body: A Guide for Occupants*,[1] that "While 95 per cent of the brain has been built by the time the owner is ten, the synapses aren't fully wired until he has reached his mid-to-late twenties!" It appears that the immaturity of the brain of young people makes them susceptible to impulsive behavior and a lack of common sense far longer than I had understood.

Donnybrook

I checked the white board and saw two patients' initials listed. They had the same complaint: injured in a bar fight. Hmm, I was intrigued.

It was a Saturday evening in December 1982. I was still working as an attending physician in the ER of the George Washington University Hospital in Washington, D.C. Our regimen specified that a student would see the patient first followed by the resident's examination. The resident would then discuss his case with me, and I would make my teaching points and recommendation. However, this evening, typical for a Saturday, the patient load was heavy and so I decided to see a few patients on my own just to speed things up.

I selected the "brawl in a bar" to go see as I suspected that it would be short and simple. I looked again at the huge dry erase board to see each patient's vital signs, what the problem was, what needed to be done and which doctor was assigned to each patient. This communication board was

1   Bryson, Bill. *The Body: A Guide for Occupants*. Doubleday, New York. 2019. Pp 62–63

a huge help to me and the other professors because we could quickly identify the most serious cases.

My first thought when I read the boarded information about the two patients injured in the bar fight was, *I'll bet they are Irish.* I picked up the two charts: BINGO! Their names: Brian Muldoon and Sean Murphy. As my heritage is primarily Irish, with a sprinkling of French and Scottish, I imagined the dynamic that may have played out between these two men.

I went into the laceration room and met Mr. Murphy.

"Mr. Murphy, I'm Dr. Chris Davis. How can I help you?"

Sean was a short, slender male with black hair and the diminutive physique that told me that he was no athlete. In a voice too loud for polite company, he pointed his finger across the room to another patient seated nearby.

"I'm here because that son-of-a-bitch assaulted me!"

"Oh really? Tell me more."

"I was at a bar having a good time with my friends. Then that shithead over there started yelling curse words at me, accusing me of having cheated in law school. We both went to Georgetown Law and graduated last June. He continued yelling at me and pointed me out to the crowd as a cheat. Finally, he threw an empty glass at me from across the room. I ducked but the damn thing hit me on the head—right here." With the melodrama so characteristic of drunks, he pointed to the right side of his head behind the ear. "I then picked up my glass and threw it at him. Bull's eye! I got the SOB on the back of the head."

"How do you feel now?" I examined the small cut on the right side of his head which might require two or three stitches. I completed the rest of the examination and found no other injuries. He became impatient with my detailed examination and told me to "Bug off." Loud, drunk and rude, he was not exactly the shining star of the Georgetown Law School.

George Washington's ER had a slick system for laceration repair. Two techs worked in the laceration room just sewing cuts and applying plaster splints. They were both former Army medics: smart, fast, experienced, very professional and a tremendous help. And they were always busy.

After speaking with one of the techs who would be sewing up Sean, I walked across the room to attend to Brian needs.

"Good evening, Mr. Muldoon. I'm Dr. Davis. I gather that it has not been a great party night for you."

Brian was tall, slender, handsome and an obvious target for any interested lady. He was quiet, respectful and had a worried look on his face. His version of the story revealed a different perspective. As we spoke, Brian was looking at the floor and speaking quietly. While he reeked of alcohol, he did not have the aggressive demeanor of Sean.

"Dr. Davis, I don't know how it happened. So stupid of both of us. I think the problem started when Sean realized that my date was his ex-girlfriend. Very drunk, he made a point of passing closely to our table as he went to and from the bar. She is a pretty girl and was dressed in a manner to get noticed. When he reached his table, he turned around and in a loud voice, proposed a toast to his "favorite slut". I lost it. I stood up and threw my glass at him. I was drinking a white Russian and so the glass was rounded on the bottom. I hit him and was delighted. My friends then intervened to calm me down. My date insisted that we leave. I turned around to get my jacket when the glass that he threw at me hit me right in the back of the head."

He then showed me a three-inch scalp laceration on the back of his head. Scalp lacerations can bleed briskly; it was going to need several stitches. The sad part was that a steady stream of blood had doused the jacket of his handsome suit.

A short time later, after the appropriate evaluation for this sort of injury was finished, both men had been sutured and were discharged with their accompanying friends. The departing comments from Sean were loud and impolite, but I was too busy to care.

Several months later, I received a subpoena to court. I was required to be a witness in the Murphy vs. Muldoon assault case. My initial reaction was:

how stupid can this get? A few days later, I asked a friend of mine who was a lawyer what this was all about.

"It's simple," he said. "Murphy wants to get Muldoon convicted of assault. Not only would that damage Muldoon's career, it sets him up for a civil suit for a damage claim by Murphy. It could be worth big bucks. Did you know that Murphy is a personal injury lawyer and Muldoon is a corporate lawyer?"

Somehow, I thought this was funny, but a waste of time, nonetheless.

On the appointed day, I took the witness stand in a D.C. courthouse. The courtroom was huge with a seating capacity of perhaps 100. This day, however, the audience seats were empty except for one conservatively dressed man in the back row.

The proceedings had been going on for several hours before my arrival. I, of course, knew nothing about what had been said previously. Of the twelve jurors, the majority were Black. Sean's lawyer didn't ask me much and so Brian's lawyer took the stage. She was a tall, slender Black attorney. Poised and relaxed, she approached me in the witness stand. She had clearly learned the art of helping put witnesses at ease in her presence.

"Dr. Davis, did you see and supervise the care of both the plaintiff and the defendant?" She went on for a while to ask the boilerplate questions to verify my credentials.

"Dr. Davis, when you met the two gentlemen on that night, would you please tell the court of your initial impressions?"

"On that Saturday evening, I reviewed our white board listing current patients and saw one case that looked like a simple one—a scalp laceration from a bar fight. Then I noticed that further down on the dry erase board next to another patient's initials there was an annotation: scalp laceration from a bar fight. I grinned and thought to myself, *I'll bet that both these patients are Irish.* I picked up the two charts and smiled to myself, their names were Muldoon and Murphy.

The lawyer smiled and asked: "Dr. Davis, what made you suspect that they were both Irish?"

With a casual smile, I replied: "I know the breed."

Slightly startled, the lawyer asked: "Would you be willing to tell the court what your heritage is?"

"I'm Irish."

To my surprise, it seemed as though the majority of jurors rocked in laughter and were shaking their heads. The judge could have gaveled the jury quiet, but he too was highly amused.

After a few more questions, I was excused. As I approached the courtroom door, the lone man sitting in the audience stood up and moved to greet me. "Dr. Davis, thank you so very, very much for your time." He shook my hand with a firm grip and held my elbow with his other. His gratitude was so sincere and so deep, I was surprised. "Your help has meant so much for our family because Brian Muldoon is our son."

After asking around among my legal friends, I discovered that Brian's dad was a senior partner in one of the most highly regarded law firms in the D.C. area. His son, currently a junior associate, was on track to become a partner too. A conviction in this silly case would most likely have ruined his opportunity to climb higher in the firm. Fortunately, the judge was able to see this case for what it was, a nuisance complaint born out of a drunken brawl between two former classmates—neither of whom had finished growing up.

Many readers I'm sure will wonder why I included this silly case. I did so because it illustrates an important feature of ER life. It is another case of immature, intoxicated males doing something stupid. STUPID!! I offer this story as a hint as to how much of an ER doc's time is tied up taking care of young males, even highly educated lawyers such as this pair, doing stupid stunts. However, looking at the bigger picture, such stupidity can present as having caused knife fights, shoot-outs, gang warfare and fatal auto accidents. Think of the needless tragic effects on their loved ones. Not every male patient in the ER would make a good church deacon. *Treating the effects of male stupidity is a huge part of an ER doctor's life.*

New Pathway:
Private Practice

Leaving Academia

In late 1982, I had been an attending physician in the ER at GW for nearly three years. I had thoroughly enjoyed the teaching opportunity and had made many friends. I had grown weary, however, of the frustrations inherent in the bureaucracy of a university hospital. At this time of tight funding, the administration was overwhelmed with budget requests. The ER needed to be modernized but every other department in the hospital was also seeking funding for their projects. At this point, I decided to pursue "private practice."

In the greater Washington, D.C. area, virtually all of the community hospital ERs were staffed by physicians that were part of one of several contract groups in the area. That arrangement made sense for the hospitals. Each group of physicians did their hiring and billing; this arrangement freed the hospitals from any responsibility for ER payroll. Also, hospital administrators preferred the flexibility to switch between any group they chose to contract with.

A new group had formed a few years earlier that had a fine reputation. The medical director, Dr. George Schweitzer (real name) was well known for his outstanding leadership skills. I interviewed with him, liked what I learned and decided to join Schweitzer's group.

Dr. Sweitzer's leadership style impressed me. For example, if a doctor was not performing well for whatever reason, he would not say, "I think that you need to fix this, and this is how." He would listen carefully to the stresses and strains with which that particular doctor was dealing. After asking empathetic questions, he would give advice by saying something like, "My sense is that this is becoming a major struggle for you. What do you think you or we could do to help in this situation?" That introductory phrase, "My sense is…" worked like magic. He was taking ownership of his feelings creating an atmosphere of caring and empathy. He was a West Point graduate before he went to medical school and instinctively knew how to lead his staff through troubled times by making them feel appreciated and valuable to the team. In subsequent years, whenever the opportunity came up, I tried to imitate that style. To be honest, I wasn't nearly as good at it as George. When I was an ER director, I would from time to time have to counsel a physician or nurse who was not performing well. Unfortunately, I often got impatient with their excuses and couldn't produce the empathy that would have helped the situation. George was amazing. Under George's leadership and working with his team of outstanding emergency physicians, I felt that I was in the best possible situation to further my ER career. The group was growing rapidly and had several hospital contracts. I rotated between two of the group's main hospitals, Montgomery General Hospital in suburban Maryland and the Reston Hospital in suburban Virginia. Sixteen of the following cases derive from this era.

Bleeding Eyes

One Friday evening in 1988, our overcrowded suburban ER erupted into chaos. In reflecting back on those times, I realize a number of factors contributed to that evening's drama.

In the late 1980s, when I worked in Maryland's Montgomery County Hospital ER which abutted the border with the District of Columbia. This period in the early 1980s had become a period of explosive population growth for this area of the D.C. suburbs. The economy of the greater D.C. area was expanding. What had been the pastoral rolling farmland of Montgomery County was being more demolished by bulldozers seemingly every day. New housing developments and shopping centers had cropped up and with them came the inevitable increase in traffic. With these economic and infrastructure changes, the nature of the population shifted too. Lawyers, consultants, accountants, entrepreneurs and other new pillars of the growing white-collar demographic had moved in and were dominating what had been pastoral serenity of several small rural communities. The pace of life increased as well. In this era before cell phones, time spent in the morass of D.C. suburban traffic caused commuters to miss phone calls, be late for meetings and late picking up the kids from soccer practice. People were short of time and very impatient.

A walk-in patient in the ER on a Friday evening had better bring a book. As the community population surged, the county hospital could not keep up with the inflow of patients; it was in serious need of modernization. It was too small, too uncomfortable and even lacking a junk food dispensing machine. Patients had difficulty accepting this bus terminal environment.

After completing his or her registration, the patient was evaluated by a triage nurse. That nurse's job was to do a limited history and rank-order the patient's problem according to a scale of non-urgent, urgent and emergent. The patient's chart was flagged with a colored tape of either green, yellow or red to enable the nursing staff to prioritize the order in which the patients would be seen.

A mother with a child with a sore throat would see the chart and indignantly ask, "Why has my daughter's chart got a green tag?" She's quite sick, can barely swallow and should be seen as soon as possible!"

The triage nurse would offer reassuring words but would quickly vanish to escort an apparently very sick patient back to the treatment area. Simply put, sick patients jumped the queue. This is when the registration clerks received the full blast of the patient's family's frustration.

"When will my daughter be seen?"

"Why is this taking so long?"

Twenty minutes later, "This place is so slow that anyone with an emergency will die waiting."

"Does the *Washington Post* know about this?"

When a stream of paramedics would jump out of the ambulances and rush into the treatment area with their acutely ill cargo, those in the waiting area were again bumped further down the queue of patients waiting to be seen. The line along the pay phones grew by the hour as disappointed and pissed-off patients and their families tried to phone in progress reports to their loved ones.

As I recall, on that noisy, crowded and tension-filled Friday evening in 1988, registration clerks at the desk were having a tough time. Outside, the rain poured down in torrents. Being in cold rain in the dark often increases a frightened patient's feeling of vulnerability and victimization. At 10 p.m., the ER waiting room had only standing room.

One of the two registration clerks was named Gladys. Older than most of the registration clerks, she had a warm patient demeanor and loved her job; she knew she played a crucial role in our ER.

Reflecting on my experience as a registration clerk in a Boston ER while in college, I asked Gladys during a quiet moment how she dealt with the anger, fear and impatience constantly directed at her. She said, "I have a very important job. As the old saying goes, 'You don't have a second chance to make a first impression.' I do my best to help patients feel welcome and to extend my sense of compassion for their problem. Their anger is like a brief summer thunderstorm. Treat them kindly and it passes quickly."

Hmm. As an ER doc, it had never occurred to me how Gladys and her team made it easier for me to treat each patient. She helped me understand how we all pulled together to help not only each patient but each other as well.

I was back in the treatment area sewing a laceration when suddenly, it sounded like the entire waiting room had erupted in a volcano of screams. I dropped the suture and headed toward the roar of sound.

Rushing back into the treatment area, Gladys nearly ran me over.

"Oh Dr. Davis, I'm so scared. There's a man…there's a man out there…" She stopped speaking and collapsed into a hallway chair. She was terrified and too short of breath to speak.

"What the hell?"

My first concern was that there was some idiot in the waiting room with a gun. Shootings in ERs are rare, but they do happen.

"Call security STAT!" I yelled to nobody in particular and dashed toward the waiting room door. I stopped for a microsecond and wondered if there was a bullet out there with my name on it. I crashed through the door. As I entered the waiting room, I saw a small group of people leaving the ER as fast as they could. Many children were screaming, most crying. I grabbed the arm of a departing man and asked, "What's the problem? Why is everyone so scared?" The man looked at me and simply pointed to the registration desk and followed his wife out.

As I approached the desk, I noted a long trail of blood leading from the ER front door towards the registration desk. In front of the desk stood a tiny man, perhaps five-foot-two and at least 80 years old. He was wearing a black raincoat and a black hat, both dripping rain water. The man had pulled the brim of the hat down over his glasses like detectives used to do in old movies. Using his elbow on the desk to hold himself up, he merely stared ahead. I saw blood streaming down his face and dripping on the floor. Concerned, I tapped him on the shoulder. As he turned to me, I said, "Sir, I'm Doctor Davis. How can I…." I stopped mid-sentence. I gently lifted his hat. Mystery man was pinching his nose, revealing a torrent of bright red blood flowing out of his eyeballs. Still pinching his nose, he turned to me with fear on his face. The blood was pouring out of his eyes so rapidly that he had to blink forcefully to see. Each blink catapulted a tiny mist of bright red blood towards me.

He extended his bloody hand to me and said, "Good evening, Doctor. I'm Harry Jenkins. It is a pleasure to meet you." Apparently, this gentleman had grown up in an environment of refinement and gracious manners.

Dispensing with further pleasantries, I quickly sat him down in the registration chair before he fainted from blood loss. I called for help and the staff quickly wheeled out a stretcher. After laying the man down, we pushed the stretcher back to a "code room." This is a treatment area fully equipped to handle a cardiac arrest or major trauma. Without a word said, the nurses promptly got him undressed, started an IV, drew blood samples for lab tests and applied oxygen using a two-pronged nasal cannula. Now the blood coming out of his eyes was festooned with bubbles.

"Mr. Jenkins, what is going on here?" I asked.

He then coughed and sprayed me with blood. "I…I…I think I have a nosebleed." His blood splattered my white coat, glasses and even my hair.

Looking quickly at each other, the nurses donned surgical masks, yellow protective paper gowns, and put on surgical gloves. They covered Mr. Jenkins in a huge protective sheet intended to absorb the dripping and flying blood. These precautions are routine to help protect the staff from exposure to blood-borne diseases.

Nurse Kinney reported in a matter of fact manner, "Blood pressure 110/60, pulse 120, pulse oxygen meter reading 94. I felt his pulse and found it slightly weak. IV saline was running to keep his blood pressure in a safe range until the bleeding could be stopped. Saline (closely related to a similar fluid called Ringer's Lactate) is diluted saltwater that has the same salt concentration as the patient's blood. The patient's oxygen level as measured by a finger probe told me that his blood oxygen level was 94%. That's a bit low but pretty good for an 80-year-old male. Hmm. I felt the fast pulse in his wrist and it was clearly weak. Clearly, he had lost a great deal of blood.

I asked one of the nurses to send off the routine labs, including a blood count, clotting studies and multiple chemical tests including those that might be needed to order a blood transfusion. One of the nurses wiped his face from top to bottom with a damp, soft cloth.

"My friend, you have a steady leak of blood coming out of your eyes and your nose. Help me understand what happened. What medicine are you taking?" Before he could answer, he sat up choking and coughing up more blood.

"I don't know, doc. I keep all my medicines in an old coffee jar with a screw top."

"Do you know their names?"

"Gosh doc, all I know is that I take two yellow pills, a large white one, a small white one and one that looks like a miniature rain barrel."

"How can we find out what those medicines are?"

"I'm sorry but I don't know. My wife would know but she is home sleeping after a hard day of taking care of the grandchildren." With a shaking hand, he reached into the pocket of his hands and pulled out a small glass jar the size of a small instant coffee jar. "Here they are, doc. Will this help?" I could plainly see several different types of medicine all combined into this one small jar. I asked one of the nurses to take the jar to the hospital pharmacist and see if he could give us some helpful information.

Concerned about Mr. Jenkins' blood loss, I tried to lower the head of his stretcher, but he sat bolt upright coughing and spitting blood. As his oxygen level was OK, the nurses removed the nasal cannula and placed a padded, plastic, spring-loaded clamp to his nose to stem the bleeding. While the plastic clamp was slowing the blood flow from his nose, the bleeding from his eyes continued. By this time, the hemorrhage had created circular bruises around his eyes, making him look like a character out of a horror movie.

We all have two tunnels that connect each of our eyes to our nose. That is why when you cry, you have to blow your nose. The tears are flowing down the tunnel. Interestingly, in this case, when the patient would pinch his nose, the blood from his nose bleed was flowing uphill and coming out both eyes. Obviously, this man's blood could not form clots.

I rolled up a small piece of gauze into the size and shape of one-half of a cigarette. I placed the role under the patient's upper lip and told him to press his upper lip as hard as he could with his free hand. This maneuver compresses the artery that feeds that part of the nose where bleeds usually start.

As I was thinking about what to do for Mr. Jenkins, I reviewed the relevant anatomy. Then my guardian angel, with some impatience, shouted into my brain: "*Wake up dude. This guy is massively over anticoagulated!*"

I performed a limited exam and then focused on his nose bleed. The results of the blood tests, including the clotting study, weren't back yet but the message was obvious. I needed an ENT tray STAT. The nurses had anticipated that need and had already set up the tray next to the bedside. Irritated by my casual response to the risk of spilled blood, the three nurses surrounded me and wrapped me in the head-to-knees protective yellow gown.

Using a piece of plastic tubing called a suction catheter, and a very bright headlight shining up his nose, I saw the culprit. A small blood vessel was freely bleeding. I could have cauterized it electrically, but that is pretty painful. So, I tried an old-fashioned method of holding a long Q-tip-like stick containing silver nitrate next to the bleeder. Silver nitrate causes blood to clot. Using the catheter to suction away blood so I could see the target, I pressed the tip of one silver nitrate stick into the bleeder; the bleeding slowed but didn't stop. After several tries, my last silver nitrate stick did the job. Whew! I then packed his nose with a long strip of gauze designed to keep pressure on the bleeding site.

The lab studies came back and showed that his blood had virtually no ability to clot.

"Mr. Jenkins, the lab results show that your blood isn't clotting. Can you help me with that? Are you taking a blood thinner?"

Then the old man smiled and chuckled. The nurses and I exchanged WTF glances.

"My doctor has me on a blood thinner. I forget the name of it."

"Coumadin?" I suggested.

"Yes, yes. That's it. I had a blood clot in my lungs a while back and he put me on that stuff."

"When was the last time you saw him? Have you had your blood clotting test done recently?"

After a brief chuckle, he confessed. "I think I caused all of this hulla-baloo tonight. I take coumadin, a blood pressure pill and a heart medicine called—I think—digoxin."

I politely pointed out, "Coumadin can cause the blood to quit clotting altogether if the dose is wrong."

The patient let out a deep sigh and then confessed.

"I ran out of my coumadin about ten days ago. Two days ago, I finally got my refill from the pharmacy. My wife was angry at me for missing my medicine. So, to get caught up, I went to the bathroom and took ten coumadin pills to make up for the ones I had missed

"All at once?" I asked.

"Yes. I'm afraid so."

"Did you take all of your blood pressure medicine and the digoxin all at once too?"

"Oh no," he explained. "I know that doing that would make me really sick."

"But didn't your doctor explain to you how dangerous it can be to take coumadin incorrectly?"

"Certainly, he did. But doctor, you have to understand that when I had those blood clots in my lungs, I nearly died. My wife is now terrified that the Good Lord will summon me before my time. And—well you know—she has an Irish temper."

Having had an Irish father, I completely understood. My dad was always either in a grouchy mood over nothing or (sometimes) feeling guilty about having been such a grouch.

The treatment for coumadin overdose is to give the patient fresh frozen plasma, or FFP as it is called. I paged the hematologist on-call, Gary Hansen. Gary called the blood bank to prepare the FFP and ordered two units of blood for a transfusion. Actually, the blood bank had started the process when they realized how out of whack Harry's clotting tests really were. Gary arrived about twenty minutes later and began the process of admitting Harry to the ICU.

While Gary was busy making the needed arrangements, Harry and I had a few minutes to chat. "Where is your wife now?"

"At home, I guess. When I got the nosebleed and it would not stop, I drove myself to the ER without telling her. The trouble was, it was hard to drive at night in the rain with blood pouring out of my eyes. Don't tell my wife about this."

I never saw Mr. Jenkins again, but I ran into one of his nurses on the medical floor. He had recovered after two days once his clotting problem was straightened out. The nurse went on to say that the real drama was Mr. Jenkins' wife. She relayed that Mrs. Jenkins was upset that her husband was afraid to confide in her and she apparently had cried for hours.

We all get a bit forgetful as we get older, sometimes running out and forgetting to take medicines correctly is a common consequence. It is not unusual for an elderly man to be on eight or more prescription medicines. Taking so many pills becomes confusing. I have always been amazed by how many elderly patients come to the ER having placed all of their medications together into a single bottle for convenience.

In 2011, the National Institutes of Health reported a study among developed countries and found that patients with chronic conditions were not taking their medicines as prescribed 50 per cent of the time! Pharmaceutical companies take years to develop an effective drug intended to make the patient better. The patient's doctor evaluates the patient's problem and prescribes the appropriate medicine. Nevertheless, thousands of hospitalizations occur for patients like Mr. Jenkins because of complications relating to incorrectly taking their out-patient medications.

Doctor, No

"Dr. Davis, please don't do it. Don't do it to me. I'll survive without it. I'm begging you, please don't do it," pleaded a critically ill pediatrician. I remember this case from the 1980s so well because it presented me with the most acute ethical dilemma I've ever had.

I was again working the night shift in the ER of Montgomery General Hospital. I preferred to work the night shift. First, by agreeing to work only night shifts, I had to work only four shifts a week instead of five. Since my wife had a busy medical practice, it gave me more free time to enjoy her company. Night shifts also had another benefit unrelated to the schedule. While there may be fewer patients coming in after midnight, they are the sickest. Heart attacks, acute shortness of breath, terrible abdominal pain, motor vehicle accidents and falls are all more likely to come to the ER after midnight. The dark of night seems to increase fear and motivate patients who are having these symptoms or situations to come to the hospital rather than wait until the next day. During a night shift, I felt that I had a greater opportunity to save lives. I had two nurses working with me, Dominique and Heather. Both were superb nurses and worked only the night shift. Heather was married to a police officer, while Dominique's boyfriend was a paramedic. Somehow, this arrangement enabled them to synchronize their schedule with that of the men in their lives. That sounds crazy but seemed to work. We worked beautifully together as a team.

On this particular night, about 4:00 a.m., the rescue unit called and reported, "Dr. Davis, this is Chris Guido in Medic 15. We are in-bound with a 58-year-old physician, a pediatrician in fact, who is extremely short of breath and his lungs sound like pulmonary edema. Had chest pain earlier but not on the oxygen. BP 90/60, P 110, pulse ox 88. He is on a non-rebreathing mask getting 100 per cent oxygen. I've given him nitroglycerine, 650 of aspirin. Because of his low BP, I haven't given him any morphine."

A few minutes later, I heard the rumble and squeak of the ambulance as it pulled in.

The patient was sitting upright on the stretcher holding the oxygen mask to his face. Perspiring heavily, he was breathing rapidly. With each breath, I could hear from across the room the bubbling sound from all that fluid backed up into his lungs.

Dominique, without a word from me, transferred his oxygen tubing to the unit on the wall which was capable of high flow oxygen. She connected him to the monitor, which showed me his pulse rate, his blood pressure, his oxygen level and his cardiac rhythm.

As the nurses did not need my supervision for any of these steps, I went immediately to talk to the patient, Dr. Mark Mateo. The patient was sitting upright on the stretcher, as any attempt to lie down made his shortness of breath severe. Able to only speak a few words without taking a breath, he filled me in on his problem.

"Chris, can I call you Chris?" he asked.

"Certainly," I replied.

"Here's my story. I'm a 58-year-old pediatrician living in Silver Spring. My cardiac history is pretty bad. I had an MI (heart attack) five years ago and was taken to Georgetown. I had a right coronary MI and had developed a third-degree heart block. So, I got a pacer. In the last year, I have had two more heart attacks. When they did the cardiac catheterization, the blockage in my coronary arteries was extensive." After telling me points about his cardiac history in between gasps for air, he stopped talking, pressed the oxygen mask to his face, and took several breaths. "Congestive failure has been my big problem since. I have PND that is getting worse. I had chest pains tonight, but they went away when I took some nitro."

What does all this mean? When he mentioned PND, Mark was referring to severe shortness of breath. Mark was describing a common history for patients with severe disease in their coronary arteries. Basically, after a patient has had a heart attack, a portion of the heart muscle is weakened. The heart muscle's ability to pump the blood to the rest of the body is impaired. Therefore, the blood starts to back up into the lungs just like a partially clogged sink. That's when things get worse. The blood back-up pushes fluid out of the blood vessels and into the lungs' small air sacs called alveoli. This leakage of fluid into the air sacs is called pulmonary edema. As the alveoli start to fill up with water, the patient's hypoxia worsens, and things can go to hell rather quickly.

To check the current condition of Mark's heart, I ordered an EKG. It can be an indicator of new heart damage. Dominique handed me Mark's EKG readout, which I studied carefully. I saw evidence of his old heart attacks but nothing new.

"Heather, would you please call respiratory therapy and tell him this patient needs PAP, STAT?" Rob Nichols, the respiratory therapist, showed up promptly. Within minutes he was delivering the crucial PAP, which stands for Positive Airway Pressure. Administered using a tight-fitting face mask, PAP increases the push of fresh oxygen into the lungs and ideally drives some of the fluid that is filling the lungs' air sacs back out into the blood vessels enhancing oxygen delivery. While Rob worked with Mark, I asked Heather to page Dr. Stout, the on-call cardiologist.

Without my notice, the x-ray tech had taken a chest x-ray with Mark sitting upright on the stretcher. The film showed the largest heart I had ever seen. The right side of the heart was pushed up against the right side of the thorax; its width was great enough to simultaneously press against the left side of the chest wall as well.

While waiting for a return call from Dr. Stout, I turned my attention again to Mark's vital signs. His blood oxygen level was slowly drifting down. He was dying.

"Heather, please set up a dopamine drip." I chose dopamine because at low doses it makes the heart beat stronger; and by carefully administering increased doses it can make the blood pressure rise within safe limits. However, whipping a dying horse may make him walk faster briefly, but not for long. So too, dopamine is an intermediary measure and does not solve the problem that made Mark this sick. Normally, dopamine is started in the ICU with sophisticated measuring equipment that makes it easier and safer to administer. However, desperate situations require desperate measures. I needed to start dopamine right away in the ER.

Heath called, "Dr. Stout is on the phone." Maurice Stout was like me, a night owl. I had never known him to be irritated when I've called at night.

"Hey Chris, Maurice here. What have you got?' I summarized the story, the physical finding, EKG, chest x-ray, positive airway pressure and his slow deterioration.

"What's the patient's name?"

"Mark Mateo," I replied.

"Oh, Mark Mateo. I've heard of him. Georgetown cardiologists have done an amazing job of keeping this guy going. This is going to be a difficult save, Chris. Have you intubated him yet?"

"I have not intubated him yet but that is next," I replied.

"You'd better hurry. I'm finishing up with a patient here at Holy Cross Hospital, but I will be there as soon as I can."

As the patient's oxygen level continued to get worse, I decided that I had to intubate Dr. Mateo in order to force oxygen into his lungs. I was planning to then put him on a ventilator, which would enable me to provide oxygen to his lungs under good control.

I turned to the nurses and said, "Ladies, please set up an intubation tray. Let's use Ketamine and succinylcholine." Ketamine is a sedative that facilitates intubation, while succinylcholine (called "suxx" by the ER staff) is a paralytic drug that prevents the ability of a patient to move, speak or even blink his eyes. It is virtually impossible to intubate patients who are awake as they will gag, vomit and clench their mouth; a paralytic medication must be given first.

By this time, Mark was becoming groggy with hypoxia and exhaustion. "Mark, things are getting worse. I need to put you to sleep and intubate you."

Immediately, his eyes opened widely and, after lifting the oxygen mask as far as he could, he cried out to the best of his ability, "Chris, please don't do it. Don't give me the succinylcholine! Don't do it to me. I'll survive without it. I'm begging you, please don't do it."

Gasping for oxygen, Mark continued, "I was in the ICU once on the ventilator. They gave me 'suxx' but nobody gave me any sedation. I was paralyzed and motionless every moment for two days. I was terrified. I was trapped in a silent panic for two days. Please don't give me the 'suxx'!"

"Mark, you will die tonight if I don't intubate you. Do you have family here?"

"Hell no. My wife left me years ago. I've got nobody."

"Do you have an advanced directive?"

Confused, exhausted and panicked, he replied, "Hell, I have no idea. I've been sick for so long I've lost track of the details."

Nothing on his chart or in his wallet indicated that he had signed an advanced directive. The advanced directive, if properly administered and recorded, gives the patient the right to refuse life-saving treatment if he wishes. Lacking the advanced directive, I had to treat him as someone who wanted to live. I was unhappy about intubating him against his will, but I thought we had to give him a chance to survive.

I looked at the oxygen monitor. "Time's up. Let's do it." After an effective dose of Ketamine sedation, I gave him 120 mg. of succinylcholine. I continued to gently squeeze the oxygen bag for about twenty seconds. By then, the succinylcholine made him as limp as a rag doll. As the respiratory therapist held his head, I inserted the blunt curved blade that enabled me to visualize his vocal cords. I was able to insert the endotracheal tube into the windpipe without difficulty. I inflated the balloon and taped the tube in place. The nurses continued to squeeze the oxygen bag until the respiratory therapist had set up the ventilator.

After a few minutes, Mark's oxygen level gradually improved. I had administered a gentle dose of dopamine that had enabled his systolic blood pressure to crawl all the way back to 100/70. Mark and I were hanging in there. I gave him a second dose of a different sedative to make sure he was asleep while paralyzed. I did not want him to think that I had betrayed him.

Dr. Stout arrived shortly afterwards. Once he arrived, I had time to reflect on what had just happened. On one hand, I was bummed. I had forced my judgment against the expressed will of the patient. On the other hand, however, with no family to talk to and no advanced directive, I could not just let him die.

About an hour later, I received a call at 5:00 a.m. from Mark's cardiologist at Georgetown, Dr. David Pearle (real name). Somehow the answering system at Georgetown had notified him of Mark's arrival. I assume Dominique or Heather had paged him. I remembered Dr. Pearle from my tenure as an ER resident at Georgetown. He was, without a doubt, the most renowned teacher of cardiology in the solar system.

We discussed Mark's case at length. I was still troubled about delivering care that an informed patient did not want. Dr. Pearle assured me that I had done the right thing. I felt that way also, but this endorsement by such a renowned cardiologist made me feel better.

After two days in our ICU, Mark was transferred to the Georgetown University Hospital ICU. He died two weeks later. I never heard from his family.

Did I have the right to give him succinylcholine against his wishes? If he had brought with him an advanced directive and refused my care, he would have died in minutes. The problem was that advanced directives are designed to end the suffering for someone whose death is inevitable. I did not think that his death was inevitable. I thought that I could rescue him. His panic about the succinylcholine was not because he thought that it was poison. In

COMPASSION AMIDST THE CHAOS

his earlier life, he had been intubated, placed on a ventilator and paralyzed but without adequate sedation. He suffered a prolonged panic attack that went unrecognized by the ICU staff because he could not talk. He was, after all, paralyzed. All of that could have been prevented by alleviating his suffering with adequate sedation. Looking back on it, I am relieved that he did not give me an advanced directive. I so wanted him to live.

Harriet with a Headache

"When you hear hoof beats, think horses, not zebras." Unless a zebra could be fatal.

When Harriet Smith's family brought her into the ER, she complained of having "the worst headache of my life." Harriet, 64 years old, had been suffering with this severe headache for the last six hours while attending the rehearsal dinner for her daughter's scheduled wedding ceremony the following day.

An ER doc usually has only one opportunity to evaluate the patient's complaint. My job was to consider all the disastrous possibilities for this symptom and rule them out sequentially. Harriet gave the classic description used by patients who are suffering a neurological disaster. Could her headache be due to a stroke or bleeding in her brain? Or a brain tumor? Or an infection? Did she have a fall striking her head after drinking several glasses of wine at the rehearsal dinner? Did the patient recently return from overseas having contracted cerebral malaria? All these possibilities could be fatal if I missed them. She denied a history of migraine. After taking the history and examining her, none of those potentially life-threatening diagnoses seemed like a reasonable explanation.

There is an old classic saying for when a doctor is taking care of a patient: "When you hear hoof beats, think horses, not zebras." That is fine advice most of the time. However, in my career I have seen and cared for: a woman with only elbow pain that turned out to be a heart attack; a male with an headache due to carbon monoxide poisoning from working in his garage the previous week with a propane heater; a man with intermittent back ache after lifting furniture that turned out to be due to an enlarging aneurysm of his aorta. All of these conditions might have been fatal had any of these patients been sent home without the correct diagnosis.

Then there is the flip side of the problem. If an ER doc spends too much time ordering too many tests chasing obscure diagnostic possibilities, the ER will get backed up, both nurses and patients will be frustrated by waiting times longer than necessary and the unusually large ER bill from the hospital follows. Such a physician would never survive as an ER doc.

During our discussion, I learned that the rehearsal dinner had been a disaster. Her prospective son-in-law made too many references to the brides-maids, several of whom he had dated. Perhaps intimately? The event planner had failed to order flowers for the dinner. Her husband had too many glasses of wine and made a toast disparaging the groom's career choice to join his dad's plumbing supply business.

After further explanation, it became apparent that the disaster was not in her brain but at the party. Harriet was "...too furious to cry." So, there you have it: a tension headache like we all get from time to time. However, circumstances made this one a doozy. Reassurance from her family and some simple analgesics made her feel better and she was discharged.

Thoroughness versus uncertainty: Learning to balance the challenge of evaluating each patient with appropriate thoroughness is constrained by the apparent urgency of the patient's problem, and by the need to simulta-neously care for other patients and to keep up with the in-coming flow of new patients. While the majority of patients do not have a life-threatening situation, impending disasters can masquerade behind common and simple complaints and symptoms. ER docs must learn to decide how thorough and detailed the patient's evaluation should be. Does the patient need an extensive group of lab tests or a CAT scan? Or an MRI at 2:00 AM? Interestingly, that decision is related in some way to the doctor's personality, which in turn, impacts the physician's choice of specialty. Emergency Medicine presumably selects for individuals with a certain tolerance for uncertainty. We have to be able to make quick important decisions frequently without as much information as we would like to have.

Before discharging Harriet, I gave her and her family the following instructions. I explained, "Ms. Smith, I have looked hard for evidence of something serious causing your symptoms. What I have found is very reassuring. However, I am not God and I cannot predict the future. You and I are in this together until you are feeling fine. I recommend that you make an appointment with your primary care doctor (or appropriate specialist) for a follow-up if the problem continues. But it is important for you and your family to return promptly to the ER if you feel that you are getting worse. Feel free to call me. Here is my cell phone number."

After Harriet and her family left, I knew they understood that I had done my best and that I cared about her. Then, I was able to go home and crash into a deep sleep. I do not know how many patients like Harriet followed my advice and subsequently returned to the ER. Phone call? I received only two phone calls from such patients. Both of them called only to thank me.

Jeremy

We called it "Friday evening's Tidal Wave." The surge of patients who come to the ER Friday evening seeking care is well known to any ER physician. Often, parents who are both working and cannot get off to take their child to the pediatrician come shortly after dinner time. Physicians in practice who are tied up with too many patients late Friday afternoon send the sick ones to the ER because they just don't have time to see everybody. When I picked up the chart for Jeremy, a seven-year-old boy with a sore throat, I was pleased as this was going to be a fast, simple case.

Jeremy was a thin young boy with tearful eyes and saliva drooling down his chin. His tight hold on his mother's arms conveyed his fear, pain and misery. His mother, who happened to be a nurse, said that he had developed a sore throat the previous day, but now had a fever, terrific pain in his throat and had trouble swallowing.

I sat down next to Jeremy who then turned and buried his face in his mother's sweater and cried softly. With gentle coaxing, he let me look in his throat. Good Lord! Terrifically swollen, two red tonsils glared back at me, both covered with a white, gooey discharge. Tonsillitis—big time. Except for some swollen lymph glands in the neck, the rest of the exam was normal. Just then an ER nurse called out to me that the cardiologist I had been trying to reach was on the phone. I excused myself to Jeremy and promised that I would be right back. Nobody in life has as many interruptions than an ER doc.

As I was talking on the phone at the nurse's station, the whole ER heard a blood-chilling scream from Jeremy's room. I slammed down the phone and dashed to his room.

What I saw shocked me. A huge column of bright red blood was pulsating from Jeremy's mouth. His mother was screaming for help and trying to hold a panicked Jeremy on to his stretcher. The blood was bright red and gushing out in fast, forceful squirts. His violent coughing was literally spraying the room with blood. This told me immediately that the bleeding was coming from a hole in a large artery in his neck. I looked inside his mouth and saw nothing but a rising gusher of pulsating bright red blood spraying upward towards me. After quickly donning sterile gloves and relying on feel only, my fingers felt a pulsatile jet of blood coming out from behind his right tonsil. Oh my God! The obvious explanation was that the infected tonsil on the right side had bored a hole into Jeremy's right carotid artery. (There are two carotid arteries, one on each side of the neck. They are large and the principle source of blood flow to the brain.) It was clear that Jeremy was going to die in a few minutes unless the bleeding could be stopped. Using two fingers and a small gauze pad, I firmly pressed down on that pumping spigot that I still could not see. The ER nurses quickly inserted two large IV lines so that we could give him fluid to maintain a blood pressure.

As I tried to compress the artery to stop the bleeding, I became worried that my finger would actually push the infection from his tonsil into the carotid artery and shower his brain with bacteria and pus. My efforts might turn Jeremy's brain into a neurological disaster. I had not been to church in decades. Gripped by fear, all of that old Catholic teaching about praying to God when you are in deep trouble came flooding back to me.

I summoned the other ER doc on duty with me, Dr. Tom Ryan (real name), who rushed into the room and positioned himself at the head of the stretcher. There Tom tried to suction out this torrent of blood so that Jeremy might be able to breathe. In this situation, saving Jeremy required inserting an endotracheal tube immediately. Jeremy's windpipe was being flooded with bright red blood. Normally, to insert such a breathing tube requires being able to see the top of the trachea, thus enabling the doctor to be sure that the tube is entering the right spot. The volcano-like geyser of blood, and my hand in the mouth plus Jeremy's thrashing and coughing made it very difficult for Tom to see the boy's trachea. Normally, the patient is sedated to make it easier to locate the landmarks in the upper airway and insert the ET tube. However, in this situation, we felt that Jeremy was at risk of drowning in his own blood in a matter of one or two minutes. Accordingly, there simply was not enough time to insert the IV and sedate him. Tom's first two attempts to insert the breathing tube failed. Third try—BINGO! Tom's tube entered the trachea. Now the nurses were able to put oxygen directly down where it belonged and stop that torrent of blood that was flooding his lungs.

"Dr. Werner Braunwald is coming down STAT," called the charge nurse. By incredibly good luck, Werner Braunwald, a vascular surgeon, heard his beeper blare "Trauma team to the ER STAT." He came flying into the room minutes later. I told Werner what was happening. I asked him if he wanted to look inside Jeremy's mouth, as my pressure on the artery had caused the bleeding to slow somewhat. *I immediately realized what a stupid idea THAT was!* He growled, "Hell no! Tell the OR we are coming!" With that, we hurried to the OR with me holding my fingers on the artery until he was placed on the OR table. Werner was in charge now and I enjoyed hearing the solid thud of the OR door closing.

A surgical nurse outside the OR approached me, handed me a towel and said, "You look like you are going to need this." Puzzled, I took the towel and sat down. Moments later, almost immobile with exhaustion, my face was buried in the towel as I fought back my tears. Then I heard the phone at the nurse's station ring. The nurse answered and called to me, "Doctor Davis, It's the ER. They need you back."

About an hour later, two nurses and an anesthesiologist were pushing a stretcher through the ER out to the ambulance entrance. Jeremy was on the stretcher, intubated and unconscious. He was quickly loaded onto the waiting ambulance for the lights and siren trip to Children's Hospital about fifteen minutes away. Without having any time to talk, the anesthesiologist gave me a grin and a thumbs-up. Werner called me and said that he had tied off the bleeding carotid artery, which stopped the bleeding. (Jeremy's brain was then relying on his left carotid artery for blood supply, which works well in young people with non-clogged arteries.) He promised to call me back with more details, but he had another patient waiting on the OR table

I remained reluctant to learn how Jeremy's case turned out. I guess I was protecting my heart; while I knew that we had temporarily saved his life, I didn't know for how long or whether my efforts might have possibly caused a brain infection.

Werner and I crossed paths in the hall about a week later as he was again dashing to the OR. As he went striding down the hall, Werner called to me over his shoulder that Jeremy was still hospitalized at Children's but was "looking good."

In the following days, I wondered: What if Jeremy had been discharged on antibiotics only to have this disaster occur in the car while going home? What if I had not had Dr. Ryan's help immediately available to me? What if Dr. Braunwald and the trauma team had been tied up in the OR?

Having graduated from MIT with a degree in biophysics before going to medical school, I would have considered myself a confirmed atheist if I had ever taken the time to think about it. This case made me ask myself if my fifth-grade nemesis, Sister Mary Angela, had been right all along about miracles.

Romance Disaster

The next chart in the "to-be-seen" rack had red tape across the clip, indicating that the patient needed to be seen right away. I hurried in the direction of a private exam room reserved for patients with a gynecological complaint. I knocked on the door and heard, "Come in."

I opened the door and saw the nurse, Jennifer, inserting an IV. The patient was lying down on the stretcher with her forehead covered with a wet cloth and groaning. Jennifer told me that her name was Sally Thompson and she had two complaints: pain in the area of her vagina and a headache.

Sally was in her thirties. Tears were running down her face. Her long, black hair was unkempt as if she had been thrashing about in bed.

"Ms. Thompson, my name is Dr. Davis. I'm sorry to see you suffering this way. Can you tell me about the problem?"

Sally lifted the wet cloth above her eyes and squinted in the bright overhead light.

"Dr. Davis, for the past week I have been having terrific pain in my female area. Using a mirror, I saw countless little sores around my vagina. They seem to keep coming out of nowhere. They feel like a dozen lighted cigarettes burning me. It hurts like crazy to pee. I assume its herpes."

"Ms. Thompson, I also understand from Jennifer that you also have a headache. When did that start?"

"It started this morning while I was doing my laundry. It started in the back of my neck and the lights seemed very, very bright. Now, I can't bend my neck."

This stiff neck symptom alarmed me. It sounded like meningitis. I immediately went to the head of her stretcher. "Ms. Thompson, this might hurt a bit so bear with me."

I put my right hand behind her head and gently tried to flex her neck. After raising her head a few degrees, she cried out in pain and begged me to stop. This symptom is classic for meningitis, which is an infection of the tissues overlying the brain called the meninges.

Meningitis is a medical emergency and treatment should start as soon as possible—certainly within one hour of when the patient arrives in the ER.

"Ms. Thompson, these are personal questions but very relevant. Are you sexually active?"

"Yes. I have a boyfriend."

"Is there any chance that you are pregnant?"

"I use birth control pills, so I don't think so."

"Does your boyfriend use a condom?"

Silence. She gave me no answer. But she wiped the tears away.

"Jennifer, please assemble the team; we need to do a lumbar puncture (spinal tap)."

"Ms. Thompson, I need to examine your vaginal area. There may be a connection to your headache."

Jennifer put Ms. Thompson in the stirrups and pulled the sheet up so that I could get a look. I donned a surgical face mask, put on two pairs of surgical gloves and a sterile paper gown. On the inner lips of her vagina were perhaps a dozen small, punched-out, very tender ulcers along with extensive swelling of the soft tissue. A speculum exam would have been too painful and was not necessary. I saw what I needed to see. She was suffering from a terrible case of herpes simplex vaginitis. Next, I needed to investigate her headache.

"Ms. Thompson, the examination of the vaginal area shows that you are correct. You have a herpes infection."

She then covered her face with her hands and, sobbing, she said: "I know. I know."

"How long have you been in this relationship?"

"About six months," she said wiping away the tears.

"We know now that patients who suffer from a case of herpes can have recurrence over time. Your boyfriend may have caught the herpes long before he met you."

She looked at me with a twinge of hope in her eyes, but I knew that nothing I said now would—or should—reassure her of his fidelity. I was on thin ice here. What if she had contracted herpes months prior to meeting her boyfriend and was having a recurrence?

Patients having their first bout of herpes symptoms can have a fever, muscle aches and a headache. However, Sally's presumed meningitis was causing the muscles in her neck to go into spasm whenever she tried to bend her neck forward.

"Ms. Thompson your headache is pretty bad. A headache with herpes is common, but not usually this painful. To be on the safe side, I recommend that I do a spinal tap."

After a heavy sigh, she said: "I get it. My son had viral meningitis last year and he had a spinal tap. Just do it."

It is important to make sure that the brain would not be at risk from the spinal tap, so I ordered a CAT scan. I also ordered not only the then main anti-herpes medication, acyclovir, but also two other antibiotics. When a potentially disastrous infection like meningitis is a possibility, the standard of care is to start antibiotics promptly before the CAT scan. That way, precious time for the antibiotics to work will not be lost. All these medications were running into her vein when she went for the scan. The CAT scan revealed no structural abnormalities, no bleeding and no signs of increased pressure. All of this told me that it was safe to do a spinal tap.

In preparation for the tap, I had her lie on her left side curled up in the fetal position. After dressing again in a sterile mask, gown and gloves, I numbed up the skin area between her fourth and fifth lumbar vertebrae. I then inserted a longer needle through this space to obtain some spinal fluid.

In just a few seconds, slightly cloudy looking spinal fluid was dripping out into the lab tubes. Normal, uninfected spinal fluid is clear. I sent the samples for analysis and culture.

While waiting for the lab results, I called the hospitalist on duty, Al Lowe. (A hospitalist is a doctor who only takes care of hospitalized patients. This enables practicing physicians to spend more time at their office seeing outpatients, which makes the whole system vastly more efficient.) By a fortunate coincidence, Al had a special interest in herpes simplex infections dating from his time at the NIH, the government research labs. He was eager to get Sally moved to the ICU. He made the point that herpes simplex can look like meningitis, but is actually an encephalitis, an infection that affects not just the lining but the entire brain. Encephalitis can have more serious long-term effects such as seizures, neurological damage and dementia. Fortunately, most patients who have their first bout of herpes simplex infection and develop meningoencephalitis usually do well and fully recover. But not all.

The lab tech called me and said, "The spinal fluid has a ton of white blood cells, mostly lymphocytes." What this told me was that Sally indeed had an infection in or around her brain. Lymphocytes are the white blood cells that are typically seen with a viral infection such as herpes simplex. This result was compatible with meningitis and/or encephalitis although it was too early to make that distinction and the treatment is the same. The lab was also checking for a bacterial infection, which can present with symptoms identical to Sally's. However, bacterial infections of the brain or its lining behave differently from viral infections and can be rapidly fatal.

Certainly, she knew that the use of a condom is essential to protect partners from sexually transmitted diseases. For reasons we can all understand, partners sometimes will decide to not use a condom because they absolutely trust the fidelity of their partner or are worried that the condom will reduce enjoyment. How long should couples use condoms to protect themselves from STDs? As every relationship is different, there is no universally applicable answer. So why did I select this story to tell you, the reader?

What particularly interested me about this case is the following: *While the list of STDs is lengthy, few couples understand that, in addition to causing dreadful pain in the woman, some of these diseases can cause infections that reach the brain causing lifelong disability.* (Winston Churchill's father died of syphilis in the brain.)

This case to me illustrates one of the recurrent conundrums people face. Let's imagine the thought processes the pair might go through when they have found an attractive partner. The time for intimacy has barged through the front door.

She thinks: "Wow, I really like this guy. But I had herpes six months ago. I'm fine now but if I tell him about that, he might be worried and emotionally slip away. Why don't I simply insist that he wear a condom?

He thinks: "Wow. She's incredibly attractive and I would like to go to the next level. But I had herpes six months ago. Should I tell her? Or, I could simply wear a condom.

She thinks: "Oh damn. If I ask him to use a condom that will make me seem like I do not trust him. Besides, most guys think that reduces their pleasure. But—OMG—he might think that I am hiding some gross disease or that I have a history of too many previous partners.

He thinks: "If I tell her I should wear a condom, she might think that I suspect she is a tramp."

She: After reaching in her purse, she produces one condom. The guy is pleased because she has clearly pre-thought about intimacy and agrees to the idea.

Most of us in healthcare agree that the discussion about the use of a condom would be better conducted in the light of day over a strong cup of coffee and not when the hormonal whirlwind comes sweeping through the bedroom door.

Mr. Buckman Hides the Truth

An hour and a half ahead of my scheduled ER night shift, I was enjoying dinner with my wife and children. The phone rang and we all knew what that meant. I picked up the phone.

"Dr. Davis, this is Helen at the ER. I am the charge nurse tonight and things are falling apart. Is there any way you could come in early?"

"Helen, sure. I have two questions: how backed up is the ER and who is the current ER doc on shift?"

"We are three hours backed up. Harry Thompson and Jeff Smithers are the docs and they are overwhelmed. The patients waiting to be seen aren't very sick, but both have been hit with heart attacks, car crashes, seizing kids and the like. They just can't seem to get caught up."

I knew from personal experience that Harry and Jeff were fast and very good. If they were drowning, no doubt the ER was hell's corner.

"I'll leave in five minutes." Helen hung up without saying another word. My family understood completely.

As I walked into the ER, I saw a stack of about eleven or twelve charts in the incoming basket.

Helen stopped me before I had time to put my coffee on the counter. "Thanks for coming in Dr. Davis. Please see this one first." She slapped the chart onto my chest and, before she dashed off to help a nurse in trouble, she whispered to me: "The guy was sitting in the stretcher with his arms folded across his chest while his wife was staring at him with clenched fists on her hips. She left to make a phone call and has not been back." Crucial intel from an alert nurse.

The "Chief Complaint" on the chart read "chest pain". The patient was in the cardiac room. I went straight to his stretcher. The patient was a moderately obese white male, 62 years old. He had arrived just a few minutes before me. The nurses already had an IV in place, a nasal prong in his nose administering oxygen, had done an EKG and had sent routine cardiac blood tests off to the lab.

"Good evening Mr. Buckman. My name is Dr. Chris Davis. The nurses tell me that you are not having a very good evening."

"Ah doc. This is crazy. There is nothing wrong with me but some indigestion. I took some antacids and now I am fine. I am only here because my wife made me come. She threatened to call an ambulance, but I wouldn't let her. So, I drove myself. Look, you guys are incredibly busy. Just let me get out of here and I will see my private doctor in the morning if the pain comes back."

I went through the litany of routine questions, which help identify a patient who might be having a cardiac chest pain.

"When did the chest pain start?"

"Oh, I don't know. Maybe two hours ago."

As I ran down the standard list of symptoms suggestive of a cardiac problem, his answer was always the same, "No." He denied shortness of breath, sweating, radiating pain, dizziness, and nausea.

He did admit that the pain was the same burning pain he had experienced for many years that responded quickly after liquid antacids. On those occasions, he said he would take a "swig" of Mylanta and soon feel fine. The nurse showed me the EKG printout. It looked normal but that never rules out a heart attack about to happen. His blood pressure, pulse and oxygen level were fine. His lungs sounded clear, and his heart and the rest of the exam was unremarkable.

As I finished his exam, I asked Mr. Buckman, "Where is your wife now?"

"Oh, I think that she stepped out in the hall to call my daughter."

I found Ms. Buckman just as she was hanging up the phone. I introduced myself, explained that I had examined her husband and asked, "When his symptoms began, how did he look?"

She took a deep breath, grabbed the sleeve of my white coat and replied, "Oh, doctor, he looked awful! He was clutching his chest, gasping for breath and said he was going to vomit. Sweat was pouring down his face and he looked very scared. I told him I was going to call an ambulance, but he objected. He is very, very stubborn."

"What happened then?" I asked.

"Well, I screamed at him that I was taking him to the goddam hospital, like it or not. I intended to drive but he insisted that he drive. While driving us to the hospital, he ran three red lights. That's when I realized that he was truly sick. Back in 1951 when I was in labor with our first son, do you think he would run a red light for me? Hell no!"

Ms. Buckman's information helped me determine that contrary to what Mr. Buckman claimed, his current pain might not be the typical indigestion he had previously experienced. In fact, Mr. Buckman's pain recurred but it was well controlled with nitroglycerin and a tiny dose of morphine. He was admitted to the Coronary Care Unit and was found to have suffered a small—but definite—heart attack.

This case is a classic example of a tricky situation ER doctors may encounter. Patients, especially older men, when they present to the ER with a problem, will sometimes trivialize their symptoms. The reason that they do so is because they don't want the physician to find anything wrong. Despite their denials, they are actually frightened. Perhaps they fear that their medical problem could cause them to lose their job as might happen if they were an airline pilot. Perhaps they feel underinsured and dread the potential cost to their family of hospitalization. There may be multiple, very understandable reasons for them to feel reluctant to help the ER physician in his or her hunt for evidence of trouble. Their reasoning is that thanks to the miracle of modern medical care, if there is actually something wrong with them, then the ER doc and staff will discover it. If the EKG, blood work, radiology studies and physical exam are all OK, then they are fine and can go home. Right?

Wrong. A doctor's ability to diagnose a problem falls apart when the patient does not give a complete, full and accurate history. An old and accurate axiom in medicine is that "Eighty per cent of diagnoses can be determined from the patient's history." When the patient becomes angry at the ER physician and staff because he thinks that his problem is minor, this commonly indicates that the patient is scared. This is a RED FLAG.

When I am taking care of an older male, I start to think like a detective. Can I trust that the patient is giving me the truth, the whole truth and nothing but the truth? Whenever possible, as I did in Mr. Buckman's case, I try to talk to the patient's significant other in hopes of getting the straight scoop before I let a potentially big problem walk out the door. The patient's partner can often be a key ally in the search for an accurate history.

A tragic example of what can happen when an older man does not make full disclosure of his situation occurred to the patient of a fine ER physician that I knew well. In 1980, my friend was evaluating a middle-aged man who complained of escalating back pain. Apparently, the patient was visiting the D.C. area, but was planning to return to his home in New Jersey the next day. His back pain was worse than normal after the long drive from New Jersey and so he came to the ER for evaluation. The patient insisted that the pain was typical of the arthritis pain that had been bothering him for years. He simply wanted some pain medicine and planned to see his orthopedist at home the next day. He refused further evaluation; he had become angry and impatient because he had to wait for his pain medication prescription. He refused to sign the standard "Left against medical advice" form and departed. Twelve hours later, he was brought back to the ER by ambulance with worsening back pain. Unfortunately, his back pain was discovered to be caused by a leaking abdominal aneurysm, which is a tear in the main artery in the abdomen. Abdominal aneurysms frequently start off as primarily back pain and are often confused with either an arthritic cause or a kidney stone. Minutes after arriving back in the ER, this patient had a cardiac arrest and died. My friend was devastated. I have often wondered how things might have turned out if the patient's wife had been at the bedside to assure the ER team that her husband's pain that time was much worse than his baseline back pain.

Vacation Souvenir

Ms. Tyler, a pleasant woman in her 40s, came into the Reston ER in Virginia one evening in 1990 complaining of intermittently painful red bumps on her forehead. She and her husband had just returned from Belize two days earlier, but the bumps had emerged the previous week. She was otherwise healthy.

I examined the red bumps on her forehead; they were each half an inch across. Wearing gloves, I gently palpated one of the lumps and found it to be firm, not soft like a small abscess. Stumped, I cleaned one of the lumps with an antiseptic solution and applied some topical anesthetic. Taking a surgical scalpel with a small blade, I very gently made an incision across the top of the first lump. The skin parted quickly with almost no bleeding. To my amazement, out crawled a creamy colored worm. I picked up the critter with forceps and, putting it on sterile gauze, showed it to the patient. She was shocked and horrified and quickly turned her head away. She asked me to show it to her husband. He looked at the squirming worm, became instantly pale and his knees buckled. He started to faint and the nurses quickly placed him on a stretcher. Moments later, he was OK.

I proceeded to open and remove what I thought were mobile larvae from the remaining sites. All came out wriggling like they were happy to get out. To her credit, the patient was now quite interested in what was happening. I irrigated the wounds and washed them, put a dressing on and put her on a short five-day course of anti-staph antibiotics.

While Ms. Tyler waited in the treatment room, I called the infectious disease specialist on call who explained to me that what I had discovered were the larvae of the botfly. Quite prevalent in Belize, the botfly, which looks like a house fly, attacks another insect like a house fly or mosquito. The botfly uses her wings (they are always female) like restraining belts and holds onto the legs of the victim insect she is attacking. Next, she dumps hundreds of eggs onto the captive bug's abdomen. The victim flies away carrying the load of eggs like a miniature WW II bomber. Subsequently, the insect carrying the eggs lands on mammalian skin, especially humans, and deposits the eggs. After burrowing under the skin, these eggs become larvae and grow. The infectious disease physician said that my treatment was spot-on. I sent Ms. Tyler home with topical skin care instructions. At her request, we put the larvae into a small box to take home in order to horrify her children.

Conquering Fear

When I awoke at 3 p.m. on a hot, humid Saturday in August of 1992, I felt a pervasive dread sweep through my body. I was once again scheduled to work the night shift at Montgomery County Hospital's ER. Working the night shift had special challenges. Hot summer nights, such as I first experienced in Baltimore as a resident at Hopkins, inspired heavy partying, heavy drinking, fighting, stabbings and shootings. But in addition, the specialists I relied upon to help me with my critical cases were usually home in bed. Sometimes, convincing the cardiologist, obstetrician or any specialist to come to the ER at three o'clock in the morning required careful, diplomatic salesmanship on my part. Here is where an ER doc's professional reputation among doctors on the hospital staff matters immensely. Being a believable, hard -working and smart ER doc helps a lot in terms of getting a sympathetic hearing from the groggy guy on the other end of the phone.

A quiet undercurrent of an ER doctor's life is fear. Such dread grows from multiple sources, the greatest of which is mismanaging a patient's care with a terrible outcome. How could that happen to a well-trained ER physician? Like so many tragedies, it commonly results from a sequence of events each of which may seem minor but with a cumulative total. Perhaps it was the result of too many patients at the same time or the patient not giving a truthful history or too many interruptions and distractions or exhaustion on the part of the physician. The list of possible contributing factors to such a tragedy is very long.

Years earlier during my first few months of emergency medicine residency at Hopkins, I had had the painful experience of calling a chief surgical resident into the ER to see what I was sure was a case of appendicitis. My patient was a 30-year-old male with nausea, vomiting, a low-grade fever and exquisite tenderness in the right lower quadrant of his abdomen. When the exhausted general surgeon came in the middle of the night only to find that my patient's pain had miraculously vanished, he exploded at me with a vengeful wrath that I will never forget.

Walter, the surgeon, yelled at me within earshot of the whole ER, "Chris, goddammit, this patient is fine and wants to go home. His belly is completely soft."

Feeling under attack, I said defensively, "Walter, I'm sorry. But he had an elevated white blood cell count and had rebound tenderness in his RLQ."

Walter fired back, "Maybe you should come with me on rounds some day and I will show you how to examine a belly. Just remember, today when you are sleeping in your bed, I will be in the OR operating and feeling like crap because you dragged my sorry ass down here at four o'clock in the morning for nothing!" He then stormed out.

I felt whacked like a baseball hit into the center field bleachers. The whole ER staff heard his rant. I was angry. No, I was furious, hurt and embarrassed. I wondered how this incident might affect me. Yuval Harari, in his famous book *Sapiens,* makes the point that the most important feature that separates humans from other animals is our ability to share a spoken language. He also stresses that the most popular form of language usage is gossip. In hospitals, the doctors' dining room is the breeding ground for gossip. After my misdiagnosis of appendicitis, I understood that my reputation in the hospital would live or die depending on the report card I was getting in the doctors' dining room.

After the fiasco with my consultation with Walter, I found myself going too far the other way. As a defense, I began evaluating patients too carefully and taking too long to arrive at a diagnosis before I did something like call the surgeon at 2 in the morning. Of course, the predictable happened. A few months later, I evaluated a 52-year-old lady with known cancer of the ovary. She had abdominal pain. My workup was impeccable. My good buddy, Dan Weinstein, took her to the OR. (This occurred before abdominal MRIs and ultrasounds were available.)

At five o'clock in the morning, having finished a most difficult operation on this patient that had bought her some time in life, Dan stopped by the ER. He waved me toward him and asked,

"Chris, can I talk to you for a minute?"

"Sure."

"Chris," Dan whispered, "That woman had almost a quart of blood in her belly. She made it through the procedure, but it was close. I think that you waited a bit too long before you called me." Aw shit. The patient was a lovely lady and too young to die.

After the end of that shift, I sat in my car too tired to drive. I sat there and thought about how Dan had rescued both the patient and me. Surprisingly, and unexpectedly, my eyes welled up with tears. I knew that I felt crushed with exhaustion but that did not explain the tears. What was the problem? After a while, my inner soul made the diagnosis: *I was getting to be too afraid of making a mistake. I was too worried about missing something.*

When I experienced dread on the humid Saturday afternoon before my evening shift at Montgomery County, it was several years after these residency experiences. Now I had much more confidence and experience. But still, I was going to be the only ER doctor on a potentially wild Saturday night. Even the best ER docs can get overwhelmed by the sheer numbers and severity of the patients' problems. At such a moment, I thought of my dad. He had suffered terribly as a POW in a Japanese prison camp during WW II. One afternoon, the Japanese discovered that he had established secret communication with another nearby POW camp. That night, dad lay on the floor of the hut and worried that he would be shot in the morning. He could not sleep. He told me: "After midnight, a British sergeant next to me heard me thrashing about. He tapped me on my shoulder and said, 'In Britain, we say that a coward dies a thousand deaths, but a brave man dies only once.'" That advice helped my dad. He told me that same story multiple times as the years went by. On countless occasions, when the challenge of the ER left me truly scared, I recalled his story. There I was—I was worried about being overwhelmed within the next few hours. There he was—worried about being executed within the next few hours.

My wife and I were enjoying a quiet dinner while the air conditioner was laboring to keep the house cool. My shift started at 7 p.m. and so I had to leave for the ER at 6:15 p.m. At exactly 5:30 p.m., the phone rang. We looked at each other. We both knew what that meant.

I answered the phone. "Dr. Davis, this is Connie in the ER. Can you come in just a little bit early? The place is wild and both Dr. Richards and Dr. Goldstein are getting run over. We are two hours behind, and the waiting room is jammed." Connie was a good charge nurse. I trusted her.

It is easy to feel sorry for yourself when you work in the mad house of an ER. One evening, the charge nurse, Connie, introduced me to a new nurse on the team. Angela Bianchi, RN, was divorced, had three children under age 10 and was working rotating shifts. Nurses like Angela for me are the real stars of the ER. Here she has to offer empathy and expertise to a group of (often complaining) ER patients and then go home, frazzled and exhausted, to offer her kids more love and attention. *Not even Hopkins was a life that tough.*

As I drove up Georgia Avenue to the ER, an ambulance went whizzing by me with lights and siren. Hmm. A quick calculation determined that I was ten minutes away from the ER. Allowing time to get into my scrubs, I knew that patient would be mine.

I pulled up to the parking lot of the hospital. The line of six ambulances all in the process of off-loading more patients extended all the way down the

ER driveway. Initially, that feeling of dread returned. But then I knew my adrenaline would rescue me. In the thick of what soldiers call a "firefight," you are so busy and so "amped up" that the fear usually tends to fade away. You don't have time to think about it.

As I walked through the waiting room to get dressed, a departing paramedic warned me, "Hey doc. Don't go in there. Run while you can!"

The night was crazy as you might expect: lacerations, bruises, cuts from the community swimming pool, chest pain from moving the barbeque (cardiac?), lots of crying kids, lots of anxious soccer moms; all of whom had been waiting for two hours to be seen by a doctor. The night went on like that for hours.

About 10 p.m., I received a radio call.

"Montgomery General, this is Medic 14. We are bringing in a very obese male from an auto crash. He doesn't look hurt, but he is yelling and screaming his head off. We know this patient from previous calls. He is a psychotic who is known for not taking his medications. We have him in restraints; we see no evidence of injury and have started an IV. His vital signs are normal. Hey, doc, you are going to be amazed by what happened. We'll be there in ten minutes. Medic 14 out."

I called out: "Connie, please prepare a trauma bed. We have an MVA coming. The medics say he is crazy. We will need the four-point restraints set up."

Shortly afterwards, the ER doors flew open and the medics trundled down the hall with a massive patient on the stretcher. He was at least 300 pounds.

At the top of his deep voice, the patient was screaming, "Oh Lord, help me! Help me Jesus! Satan has me in prison. I need to get away. Help me, Lord."

The entire staff assembled around the stretcher awaiting orders. Interestingly, he was yelling for rescue, but did not seem to be fighting us.

"OK, let's move him to the stretcher on the count of three." Six of us lifted him onto the hospital stretcher.

One of the paramedics spoke up, "Doc, I've taken this patient in no less than four times. He is a schizophrenic who is cared for at St. Elizabeth's Psychiatric Hospital in D.C. He gets like this when he runs out of his meds."

The paramedic paused to catch his breath, "Here's the story. Tonight, this guy was driving his car north on Georgia Avenue, in D.C. at some 80 miles an hour. Running red lights. Running stop signs. Weaving like crazy. D.C police gave up their chase when he crossed into Maryland. Once he crossed the Maryland state border, three Montgomery County police officers, all in separate squad cars, took up the chase. Being pursued by three cop cars all with blazing lights and sirens didn't faze this guy a bit. After a two-mile chase, I guess that the cops had been able to slow him down a bit, maybe to 40 mph. Then, one cop pulled his squad car against this guy's left front fender to try to push him onto the sidewalk. This nut rammed the cop car, backed up and took off again. Another cop bashed his squad car into the left side causing that car to spin with the rear wheels onto the sidewalk. He tried to back out and ram another police car that had wedged in behind him. All three of the cops ran to this guy's car, jumped this guy and tried to hold him down. He was fighting like a raging bull: swinging his fists, kicking the police officers. All this time he was yelling for the Lord to help him fight off Satan. Somehow, the cops were able to get him down on the sidewalk and restrain him. They held him down until we got there. Man, you should have seen the damage. All three police cars are totaled."

I asked the paramedics what condition the patient was in when they arrived. One paramedic said with amazement, "He was jumping and flailing around and yelling for the Lord Jesus to rescue him from the devil and all that sort of stuff. But, doc, when we got this guy into the back of the ambulance, he looked great! After three car crashes and having been taken down by three cops, I didn't see a scratch on him!" We saw no blood, there was no apparent tenderness in his chest, belly or extremities. He was just yellin' and hollerin' for the Lord to rescue him. Man, I can't say the same for the cops. They are pretty beat up."

I examined the patient thoroughly. His head, face, neck, chest, abdomen and extremities all showed no injury. Going over him inch by inch, I found no tenderness, no deformity, no lacerations and no bruises. He tried to resist my examination as he thought I was Satan about to kill him. Satisfied that he was in good shape, a gentle dose of a sedative got him to stop yelling at full volume in the ER.

A short time later, the three Montgomery County police officers arrived having been driven to the ER by one of the medic units that had answered the call. All the officers were in their twenties, two males, one female. They were a mess following the melee with the patient. Their uniforms were torn, and they had multiple abrasions and scratches. One officer's badge had been ripped from his shirt and was dangling from his pocket. The female officer was shaking like a leaf in a hurricane, but she was receiving lots of support from the other officers and paramedics.

One of the three injured officers with two stripes on his torn sleeve was apparently the officer in charge. I introduced myself and learned that he was Ralph Bates with the Montgomery County Police Department. I asked him what had happened, as I was concerned that the patient might have a significant injury that I was missing.

Soaked in sweat and totally exhausted, he told me the details of the "take down" of the patient. "When we tried to extricate him from the car, his yelling for Jesus made it clear to us that he was psychotic. He was not wearing his seatbelt. When we opened the door, he started kicking us with his boots. He then leaped out of the car and started grabbing and swinging with his fists. Somehow, he got Sandra in a headlock. Mike and I were able to pry Sandra free and then he started swinging at us. Sandra gave him a short squirt of mace. All that did was to convince him he was being attacked by Satan. Mike got pushed down hard onto the concrete curb. At this time, the fire department had arrived, and they were able to help us get him restrained and belted onto a stretcher."

The paramedic then chimed in, "Doc, you should see the scene. Three police cars and a sedan all wrecked. It's a steaming junkyard down there."

A senior officer from the police department arrived and took detailed histories from the officers. When he was done, I approached the three police officers and told them they should register as patients to be evaluated and treated. However, all three said that their wounds were superficial and that the medics had treated them in the ambulance. They all desperately just wanted to just go home. Ralph, the oldest officer, replied, "Ah, not to worry. I'll be sore in the morning, but I'm OK."

Despite their objections, I insisted that all get registered as patients, put in hospital dressing gowns and placed each on a stretcher so I could examine them. They all seemed to have scratches and abrasions, which the nurses dressed with great care, but none showed any evidence of a serious injury. I was sure that the next day they would all show a significant group of bruises. The supervisor told them all to report to the PD clinic tomorrow for a follow-up evaluation.

I watched transfixed as the three of them slowly shuffled down the hallway to leave the ER. As they chased this wild man driving his car through an intersection filled with pedestrians, these young cops had put their lives in tremendous danger. Yet, they did not club or shoot this wild and crazy man who would have been happy to kill all three of them. Exhibiting courage and professional restraint, they were teammates in a fight for their lives. They were protecting the civilians of Montgomery County; citizens who might never fully appreciate what they had done. They had been so careful with the patient. Yet, they all had been so afraid.

In the future, just by thinking about these three, I was able to dial down my own sense of fear. They had given me a yardstick whereby I could calibrate my own anxiety and keep it from running away with me. Were these police officers at serious risk doing their job? Yes, indeed. Was I likely to get seriously injured or killed doing my job? No. Clearly, President Delano Roosevelt got it right when he said: "All we have to fear is fear itself."

The Unusual X-Ray

On one particular evening in 1985, I was working the evening shift at the Reston Hospital. This hospital, located in the Virginia suburbs near the District of Columbia, was new, modern and well-staffed. Most of the patients I cared for were financially comfortable and enjoyed the typical benefits of a modern suburban life. I had spent many years in urban hospitals taking care of those suffering a life of grinding poverty. For those interested in quantifying the disparity of wealth in America, comparing ERs is a good place to start.

The brief summary at the top of my next chart stated that the patient was a Hispanic man in his mid-thirties suspected of smuggling cocaine. The police had brought him to the ER after they had arrested him at the Dulles Airport as he stepped off a flight from a Guatemala.

Luckily, when the police arrived, the flow of patients being discharged roughly balanced the number coming in to be seen—busy, but not out of control. The patient escorted by the police stood out among the evening's admissions.

The ER lights shone brightly, the ER was immaculately clean and tidy, and the "crash carts" were stuffed with every conceivable emergency drug. But, to my surprise for a modern ER, the stretchers were only separated by curtains that had to be pulled on a rack around the stretchers. Both the nurses and the ER docs valued efforts to protect privacy when talking to patients and their families. On the other side of the curtain along the line of stretchers, eavesdroppers carefully listened in to the conversations behind nearby curtains. A garrulous teenager surrounded by his fed-up parents wouldn't be surprised in subsequent days when his story was the gossip of the high school cafeteria.

This particular night, patient privacy became an issue. Carrying the young Hispanic man's chart in my hand, I walked to his stretcher and pulled back the yellow curtain. As I approached the right side of the patient's stretcher to examine him, on the other side of the stretcher stood a police officer with such monster biceps that he looked as though lifting his arms might tear his shirt. Standing six foot two, weighed down with weaponry and body armor, he looked as welcoming as a grizzly bear.

"Will you be the doc taking care of this patient?" he asked as he lumbered around to join me on the same side of the stretcher. He immediately whipped out his notebook to record the name on my badge.

Having not yet completed my physical exam of the patient, but noting his badge, I answered with a "Yes. It appears so."

The hefty officer explained, "This suspect was picked up at Dulles on a tip that he was smuggling cocaine. As he speaks no English, we had Officer Gutierrez interview him. We found no drugs in his luggage or in his clothes. We suspect that he is probably a packer."

I thought to myself, *a packer?* Having not a clue what a packer was, I did not wish to disclose my naiveté to this grizzly and so I faked an understanding nod and continued my examination.

By this time, the other police officers were standing at the foot of the stretcher enjoying the coffee provided by the ER staff and quietly chatting. The four police officers standing next to one patient created a buzz of excitement in the ER. Passers-by tended to loiter a bit near the stretcher; their ears cocked to pick up some gossip-worthy scoop.

The patient/suspect wore an open-at-the-back hospital dressing gown and was lying flat on the stretcher instead of being raised to a more comfortable incline by the adjustable upper portion of the mattress. I had learned long before that this position made the prisoner feel more vulnerable and less likely to cause trouble. A quick glance at his face told me a lot. His face blazed with terror as his eyes darted around the ER. Fat and sweaty, he groaned intermittently and rubbed his hands on his abdomen. As I could not speak

Spanish, I summoned a Hispanic nurse named Maria to help translate. Of the many mistakes I made in college, not learning Spanish stands at the top of the mountain of stupidity. Everyone in healthcare needs to be able to speak Spanish. Sweet and hard-working, Maria was adored by the entire ER staff. Because she was short, she could speak to the patient in Spanish at eye level.

"Maria, I need your help. Is this patient having any pain, shortness of breath, fever, nausea...?" Maria knew the question sequence as though she had been practicing it for years. Maria spoke to the patient in a warm, compassionate voice and then shared with me, "This man is from Guatemala. His name is Javier Sanchez. He came here to see his family in western Maryland. He, at first, told me that he felt good and that nothing was wrong but then he rubbed his stomach and said his abdomen hurt. He does not want to tell me much because he knows that Officer Gutierrez here understands what he is saying."

Delicate problem. Interviewing a patient who is under arrest is always a problem for ER docs. I was worried that my line of questioning would cause the patient to disclose criminal activity; by now the police were not around the stretcher, but just outside the curtain. What about his privacy? His rights to a lawyer? The Miranda warning? There is a difference between getting a clinical history and interrogating a patient. I was simultaneously remembering some cases where bad guys who felt that I was interrogating them had fled from the ER without treatment suspecting that the police were closing in.

I checked Javier's vital signs. His pulse was a bit fast, but his BP was OK. I had him sit up so I could listen to his lungs and check his back. Javier suddenly let out a groan of pain and rubbed his abdomen. I switched my focus to his belly. His belly was distended and diffusely tender. Wherever I pressed, he grabbed my hand to push it away.

When it comes to abdominal pain, there are two classical presentations to consider. If the patient is suffering from blood or pus floating about in the abdomen, that roaring inflammation causes agonizing pain whenever the abdomen is moved. Rocking the pelvis is excruciating. Pushing the abdomen and then suddenly releasing the examining hand causes terrific agony. This finding is called "rebound tenderness." Although painful to the touch, under a gently applied stethoscope, the abdomen is quiet. No bowel sounds can be heard. Almost invariably, such a finding demands a trip to the OR. On the other hand, if the abdomen is diffusely tender to the touch or distended but without localized pain or "rebound tenderness," like Javier's seemed to be, the situation is less clear. Here the stethoscope helps tremendously. If the physician hears through the stethoscope intermittent rushing sounds, called "hyperactive bowel sounds," that suggests that the bowel has become blocked for some reason. Bowel obstruction causes the contents of the gut to get backed up like traffic on a freeway. The gut tries to overcome the obstruction with a surging contraction in hopes of opening the blockage. Each contraction hurts. As I listened to Javier's abdomen, what I heard was low pitched gurgles of air interrupted by a rushing sound like a large pitcher of water that had suddenly tipped over.

Javier must have felt like his abdomen was going to explode. He was suffering agonizing abdominal pain and I presumed was terrified about being under arrest. Was he worried about leaving behind a wife and children who might no longer have any reasonable source of income?

Maria said, "His pain is getting worse." Just then, Javier vomited a very small amount of yellow fluid. Now he was writhing on the stretcher. This actually is a reassuring sign. It implies that there is no irritating fluid floating free in the abdomen like blood or pus. If there had been, moving would be too painful.

"Call x-ray. Tell them I need a flat and upright of the abdomen STAT. Be sure to send a nurse to x-ray with him and bring him back immediately if he crashes." All four of the police officers trailed the nurse and Javier on the way to x-ray. I was unhappy to see him wheeled to x-ray followed by four police officers because that gets the small x-ray room too crowded for the x-ray tech to work quickly.

"Excuse me, gentlemen, only one of you can go to x-ray with him."

"What's that about?" growled one of the officers.

"We only have enough lead aprons to cover the nurse, the patient, the x-ray tech and one other person." The officers' uncomprehending looks told me that my message had not resonated. "So, exposing your gonads to a blast of x-rays without a lead apron won't help your manhood." Only one officer went to x-ray. I then dashed to see other patients.

After ten minutes or so, the rattle of Javier's stretcher returning from x-ray caught my attention. Surprisingly, the radiologist, Sam Collins, was following behind carrying two x-rays in his hand. We both walked into a small, dark room adjacent to the ER where x-rays could be viewed. We were doing our best to provide some privacy and prevent additional eavesdropping. Good luck.

Sam wedged the films onto the view box and called out to me. "Hey Chris. Take a look. This is pretty hard to believe."

After fumbling to find my reading glasses, I moved closer to take a look. "Oh my god, what is that?"

What astonished us both was that the entire abdomen was filled with small balloons. Too many to count! Sam nailed it. "They are all condoms filled to the top with illegal drugs—probably cocaine. This is the third case like this I've seen. But even then, I could only see two or three condoms. Here his entire bowel is packed stem to stern with them."

Officer Gutierrez wandered over to the film view box. The officer let out a quiet whistle. "Holy shit! That's the biggest load of gummy bears I've ever seen." Gutierrez obviously knew a lot more about this that I did.

"Please tell me more," I asked.

Gutierrez went on. "You see, doc, in Guatemala, the drug lords have found a great way to get cocaine into the States. They find some guy with a legal passport who has family in this country. They tell him, "Don't worry. It is quite simple. We will pay you $200 if you help us out and we will fly you to the States. All we want you to do is to swallow this rubber that has a powder inside. When you get to the States, just poop it out into the crapper, rinse it off and call this number. The more rubbers you give back to our team, the more money we will pay you."

"This poor SOB," commented Sam. A couple other docs had joined us around the view box, but none of us could count all of the condoms on the x-ray. Some counted thirty. After viewing the lateral x-ray, others claimed a few more. "Hey Chris," said Sam, "you've got a helluva problem. What is a rompin', stompin' macho ER doc going to do in a case like this?"

I stared at the x-ray and said nothing. After a while, I told Sam, "These are our choices. I have no idea how much cocaine gets packed into a condom but surely it must be a massively lethal dose. If we do nothing, the high pressure in his bowel will rupture one of the condoms and he will die. Or his bowel might rupture in which case he would die." Sam and I agreed that I needed to talk to both the general surgeon and gastroenterologist on call to get advice.

I called James Sullivan, the general surgeon, on call. I liked James. He was from San Antonio, extroverted, spoke Spanish, slightly loud, but was smart, kind and, like all good surgeons, worked his butt off. James made the point that if he operated to retrieve the condoms, a tiny nick into a rubber with a scalpel would kill the patient. His judgment and experience prevailed, "Keep me posted and let me know if you need me."

Javier was admitted to the ICU where I no longer had responsibility for this care. I heard subsequently that the gastroenterologist had treated Javier very gently at first with small liquid doses of "personal lubricant" delivered rectally. A few condoms reportedly came out. A gently escalating dose of laxatives followed. Shortly thereafter, things got better. However, it took five days to empty out all of the condoms.

The rookie police officers, stationed with Javier for five days, were assigned the job of collecting all of the evidence. Reportedly, the nurses took a motherly pity on these young fellows and they did not suffer. The same could not be said for Javier. All of the pain medicines available were considered too risky, as they might slow the bowel's contractions or risk bleeding.

Of the thousands of x-rays that I saw in my career, Javier's x-ray stands alone as the only one my brain still recalls in minute detail. Javier was an indigent Mayan with a family in Guatemala, desperate for money. But whenever I roll back the chain of causality, I always come to the same conclusion: all of this was driven by the insatiable demand of Americans who use cocaine, the merciless greed of the drug cartels, and the impoverished conditions that led Javier to risk everything for a chance for a better life.

The Ultimate Heartbreak

No heartache in the ER compares to the needless, accidental death of a child. Though it was many years ago, I vividly remember the details of such a case—one that occurred largely due to the failure of nearby adults to act.

Autumn in Northern Virginia brings trees exploding with color, chilly breezes and the youthful excitement of the football season. In October of 1993, while working at the upscale Reston ER in Virginia, one of the perks was that nearly every patient who came to the ER on a Saturday night had established relationships with a host of doctors. Cardiologists, OB/GYNs, dermatologists, ophthalmologists and, of course, plastic surgeons formed a team ensuring that each patient in this community received the latest in comprehensive and expensive care. The nurses were first-rate and went out of their way to form cordial relationships with the patients and their families.

One evening shift at about 8:00, my conversation with a mother about what to do about her child's dreadful case of poison ivy was interrupted by the crackle of the fire/rescue radio.

"Reston ER, this is Paramedic Conklin on Medic 9. We are coming to your ER with a 16-year-old male in full cardiac arrest. When we arrived at the scene, the patient was apneic (not breathing) and pulseless. We started CPR immediately, but found the patient hard to ventilate with a mask. I tried to intubate the patient and I immediately saw a bolus of food blocking the airway. Using the McGill forceps, I was able to pull out a chunk of food—cheeseburger. The patient is intubated now, I hear good breath sounds over both lungs and we are doing chest compressions. We'll be there in three minutes."

"Medic 9, this is Dr. Davis. I copy."

The nurses and I exchanged apprehensive glances and quickly assembled in the cardiac arrest room. This is trickier than it sounds, as the nurses had to drop what they were doing for other patients in order to hurry to the "code" area. The ER had two "code" rooms that were elaborately equipped with the gear necessary to save a patient who is just about to die. In these rooms, positioned just to the left of the stretcher was a huge, steel "toolbox" like something you would find at Home Depot. Each drawer had specific equipment to handle any part of a rescue effort. Airway tubes, medications, IVs, defibrillation pads and a host of other necessities all were stored in clearly marked drawers allowing fast access for reviving a dying patient.

Getting ready to manage a cardiac arrest requires teamwork. I quickly gave orders to the nurses. "Janice, please continue CPR. Carol, the patient is intubated so please bag the patient with 100 per cent oxygen. Martha, I'm sure the medic unit has established an IV. Stan, please have the defibrillator standing by and ready to go. Martha, please be the scribe."

I had barely finished making the nursing assignments when we could hear the wail of the ambulance siren. The ambulance came to an abrupt and the paramedics moved the stretcher out of the back of the ambulance onto the pavement. The paramedics immediately resumed CPR and hurriedly wheeled the gurney into the ER. Through the ER entrance we saw a stretcher bearing a teenage boy receiving chest compressions. The paramedics shifted the patient onto the hospital ER stretcher in the code room and the well-rehearsed team of nurses quickly and silently went to work.

Mike Conklin, like virtually all of the paramedics in Northern Virginia, was a top professional whose paramedic career had been preceded by years as a Navy medic assigned to the Marine Corps. I had known Mike better than most paramedics, as we enjoyed sharing stories about being a caregiver in the military. Tall, and lean, his full shoulders and trim gut showed that Mike worked hard to maintain that physique so characteristic of former marines. As the nurse continued the CPR and connected the patient to the monitoring equipment, Mike told me about the case. Unusual for Mike, he was clearly upset and angry.

While Mike and I were talking, the nurses continued CPR and quickly connected the patient to the cardiac monitor where the rhythm of his heart could be followed on a black monitor screen with a bright, clear green tracer signal. The monitor signal tracked the CPR and would jump up and down as the compressions were being administered. After two minutes of CPR, I told the nurses, "Stop the CPR." I checked for a palpable pulse by feeling the artery in his neck. No pulse. As I watched his chest carefully, there was no evidence of the patient trying to breathe. We resumed CPR with ventilations through the tube located in his airway and continued to hope for a miracle.

When the heart is not beating at all, there is no value to delivering an electrical shock. On the other hand, when the heart muscle is quivering and trying to beat (the technical terms are ventricular fibrillation or ventricular tachycardia), sometimes the electrical shock will bring the heart back to a normal rhythm. Sadly, the cardiac monitor showed only a flat line.

After two minutes, I stopped CPR briefly to feel for the patient's carotid pulse in his neck. I felt nothing.

"Please continue CPR and give him one milligram of epi IV." Epinephrine is a powerful cardiac stimulant. On very rare occasions, the epi helps. In this instance, it had no effect. After forty minutes or so of trying to bring this dead youngster back to life, including multiple doses of epinephrine, I stopped the resuscitation and declared him dead. A deep silence descended on the entire ER staff. Most of us had children too.

I then turned to Mike, the paramedic. He usually displayed a calm, routine demeanor despite years of facing life and death emergencies almost daily. But this time, I could see that he was fighting to control his tears.

"Dr. Davis, this one really sucks. We were called to an evening church group meeting for the youths of the parish. The patient is a 16-year-old named Jeff who was eating a cheeseburger when, according to eyewitnesses, he grabbed his throat and could not talk. Several of the parents at the meeting were startled and did not know what to do. As he grew increasingly short of breath, he turned to several adults for help. He clearly had an airway obstruction from the hamburger as he was grabbing his throat. When no one came to help him, he tried to give himself the Heimlich maneuver by bending his abdomen over the back of a chair. After a few minutes, he appeared blue and collapsed on the floor. Again, no one offered the Heimlich. 911 was called. When we arrived, the lad was cyanotic and pulseless on the floor. We started our cardiac arrest protocol. Based on the story, I assumed that he had food obstructing his airway. I opened his throat with the intubation blade. I was able to suck away some vomit and get a good look at his trachea. There was a piece of cheeseburger wedged just below the vocal cords. I grabbed a curved clamp and with some difficulty was able to pull out the chunk of burger. We put in the endotracheal tube and got good ventilation. But he was blue, pulseless and unresponsive. While the crew continued with the resuscitation, I took my flashlight. I shined it into his eyes and his pupils were fixed and dilated."

When healthcare providers are trying to resuscitate a cardiac arrest victim, flashing a bright light into the eyes of the patient tells a great deal. Normally, when a bright light enters the eyes, the pupils constrict. We all experience this when we walk outside on a bright, sunny day. The pupils constrict down in size to reduce the amount of entering light thereby mitigating our "bright light" discomfort. However, for the pupils to have this protective reaction, the signal has to come from the brain. With rare exceptions, the failure of the pupils to constrict in the face of a direct bright light means that the brain is dead. The patient is dead.

This previously healthy teenager died from choking on a cheeseburger because not one of the youth leaders recognized the problem or knew what to do.

"Doctor Davis, this story gets worse. All of the kids in this youth club had taken the church-sponsored first-aid course, which included the Heimlich maneuver. In fact, the instructors who had taught them the Heimlich were there! They just seemed to freeze. They were paralyzed with fear and so could not...or did not...do anything to help."

Mike quietly drifted outside to the ambulance bay where his partners were reloading the ambulance. In the faint light, with his back turned to me, I could just see Mike's clenched fist bang the side of the ambulance. He carried the burden of having futilely tried to save wounded Marine Corps buddies in Vietnam. As a Northern Virginia paramedic, whenever he took care of a dying young person, I suspected that he could still hear the screams of his dying friends in Vietnam being torn apart by enemy gunfire. The fact that he continued as a paramedic in civilian life I felt was a testimony to his Marine Corps courage.

The nurses told me that the adults who had been at the scene were assembled in the family support room. I entered the room and quietly closed the door.

"My name is Dr. Davis. I am the emergency medicine doctor who has been working with Jeff. Please help me understand what happened."

"Dr. Davis, the paramedics told us Jeffrey has died. Did he choke to death?"

I knew that this case might have a legal dimension associated with it and so I was circumspect in my meeting with them.

As the paramedics had already told them that Jeffrey was dead, I saw no point in being evasive. "Yes, gentlemen, I am sorry to report that Jeffrey is gone. It appears that he died at the scene based on what the paramedics have told me."

I did not want to devastate them by emphasizing what they had failed to do—even though it was clear what had happened.

"I have no certain proof of the cause of death, but he might have choked on some food. However, that final determination will be up to the coroner."

Our conversation was interrupted when I heard one of the nurses' call, "Dr. Davis," Jeffrey's parents are here." She had brought them into a second family support room right next door.

I asked the two gentlemen to leave so that I could talk to the family. As I joined Jeffrey's parents, his mother, a well-dressed woman in her forties, was seated next to her husband. He held her right arm. Her whole body was shaking with a face contorted in terror. I started to tell the story as gently and tactfully as I could, but she interrupted me.

"With a quivering voice, she asked, "Is Jeffrey dead?"

With a soft nod, I told her that Jeffrey was dead.

An instant later, she jumped to her feet and let out the loudest, most blood-curdling scream I had ever heard. She screamed, pounded the wall, continued screaming and collapsed to the floor. Two nurses rushed in to help. She did not cry. She did not weep. She screamed and screamed and screamed. She pounded her fist against the wall of the counseling room, knocking off the table lamp, which went crashing to the floor. She then ran to see Jeffrey.

"Where is he? Where's my Jeffrey?"

There, in the soft overhead light, the ghostly shadow of her dear son lay motionless. He was still connected to monitor lines and the breathing tube inserted by the paramedics remained affixed and taped to his face.

I will never forget what happened next. She rushed up to Jeffrey's body, slapped him on the face and screamed, "How dare you do this to me? You are my son. You can't leave me like this!"

She then shook his body so violently that a nurse had to hold him lest he be pushed off the gurney. She pounded his body with her fists and then pulled herself tightly to him and placed her sobbing face on his chest.

I stood next to Jeff and his mother for a minute or two and realized that she could not hear my words of empathy. I felt emotionally exhausted. Her husband, also demolished, approached her and held her as best he could. I drifted outside to the ambulance bay into the cool autumn evening to take a few deep breaths. The paramedics were packing up their gear when Mike motioned me over.

"Dr. Davis, this is a catastrophe for everyone who knew him; he was a friend to everyone. Outside in the ambulance bay, I saw the two fellows from the church with whom I had spoken. They were holding hands and praying. I felt a deep lightning bolt of anger flash through me and with it came the thought, *dammit fellows, can you think of something else that you could have done for Jeffrey that would have mattered?*

The memory of this case has never left my heart or my head. (As I am writing this story tonight, yet another cloud of melancholy memory settled over me. I had to stop my typing, close my eyes and wait for the ache to pass.)

As I matured in my career, I encountered more and more cases of tragedy that could have been avoided by timely action of bystanders who had been trained to know what to do. What happens in these situations? Not uncommonly, individuals panic at a time like this. They may have been trained; however, in the heat of the moment, a thunderstorm blasts through their brain. Fear and confusion block their memory of what is the right thing to do. A choking victim, a drowning child, a cardiac arrest: all can create immobilizing fear in those best qualified to help.

The military understands this tendency to be paralyzed in the face of crisis and they train their personnel to compensate for it. When I attended water survival school as an Air Force flight surgeon, the instructors taught us the 10-step procedure of how to safely eject from a fighter jet about to crash into the ocean. Accordingly, no student could graduate from the course without accurately reciting to one of the instructors the 10 steps of the "ejection-over-water" procedure over *thirty times*. I still remember the 10 steps.

Though I am retired as an emergency medicine physician, I routinely teach Advanced Cardiac Life Support and Pediatric Advanced Life Support courses developed by the American Heart Association. These courses teach information and techniques to those medical providers who primarily work in emergency departments and intensive care units as well as those who only rarely encounter such emergencies. My goal is to help this latter group keep their wits about them when they are confronted with the sort of emergencies they do not see very often.

As you can tell, my sadness for Jeffrey's family has never left me. Our son had a close friend with whom he grew up named Robert. This young fellow, a warm, funny, gregarious athlete, was at our house most of the time our son was home; both boys constantly raided the refrigerator. Over the span of nearly a decade, he became another son to my wife and me. A hidden IED killed him in Afghanistan. His death stands alone as the greatest heartbreak I have ever felt. Robert's tragedy helped me develop a new appreciation for the importance of expressing empathy. Empathetic doctors can help speed the healing of those who need it most. As every doctor knows: "The most important part about caring for a patient is caring about the patient." That said, sometimes the doctor needs empathy too.

Wedding Disaster

I picked up the chart and read, "Chief complaint: swallowed pins." It was 4 p.m. on a warm Saturday and the pace in the Reston ER was slow.

The patient had been brought to the only room in the ER with a door. I knocked gently on the door and said, "Hello. I'm Dr. Davis. May I come in?"

Hearing a prompt "Yes," I entered. In front of me on a stretcher sat a beautifully dressed young woman in her mid-20s. She had shoulder length black hair, high heels, and was wearing an assortment of gold jewelry that adorned a dark red dress. No one dresses up to go to the ER, so this was unusual.

"Good afternoon, Ms. Morelli. How can I help you today?"

"I have a stomach full of sharp pins," she replied. She seemed calm, relaxed and not particularly upset. She stood up off the stretcher to shake hands with me but certainly was not smiling. Turning, she introduced the two older adults standing behind her as her parents.

"Tell me more," I asked.

She started off with a deep sigh that I often saw in a patient who was short of breath or really pissed off. "Dr. Davis, I am supposed to be the maid of honor at the wedding of my best friend. The ceremony is starting now. About an hour ago, I was helping one of the bridesmaids with her dress. It seemed to have a baggy shoulder and I wanted to tighten it up for her so that the seamstress could put a few stitches in it. I was using a few straight pins to adjust her dress. In fact, I had four straight pins in my mouth. Just then, one of the groomsmen gave me a cheerful slap on the back and told me how fabulous I looked. Startled by his endearing slap, I swallowed all of the straight pins." As she told her story, her arms were folded and her generously applied red lipstick had become a grim, thin horizontal line. I couldn't help thinking she might already be planning some sort of revenge.

I left the treatment room and contacted the gastroenterologist on call, Tim Johnson, whom I knew; I explained the situation. He was a bit grumpy and for good reason. Outside, the Saturday sunshine was a stronger lure than trekking to the ER. When he arrived, he gave me a silent wave, picked up the chart and went to see the patient. Cheered by the fact that he could really help her, he returned to the nurses' desk and placed a call to summon the OR team.

About one hour later, Tim and a nurse took Ms. Morelli to the operating room. After the anesthesiologist had put her to sleep, Tim looked into her stomach using a flexible, fiberoptic scope. Later, before going home, Tim stopped by the ER and told me, "Boy, I sure was lucky. Each of the pins had a small red top. They weren't hard to find and the pincer on the scope made them easy to pull out. By the way, one of the nurses cleaned the pins and put them in a small box. She gave them to the patient as a souvenir."

The maid of honor spent the night in the hospital recovering from her anesthesia. The groomsman's whereabouts might still be a mystery.

The Brilliant Psychotic

On a chilly night in November in about 1994, the rescue squad brought in what certainly appeared to be a vagrant into the Reston Hospital ER. The odor of the patient's body filth was overpowering. Having found him walking aimlessly in the middle of the street in the dark, the police called the rescue squad to take him to the Reston ER. When he arrived, he smelled so badly that the nurses insisted on putting him in a room where the door could be closed. He had no family, no wallet, and no identification. Obviously, he was homeless.

I was disgusted. Even though this Saturday evening shift was in a modern, well-appointed ER in the suburbs of Washington, D. C., once again I was faced with another unwashed, unkempt street person, possibly a drug addict, whose needs push the limits of my patience and society's safety net.

I put on an OR gown to protect my clothes and donned not one but two pairs of sterile gloves and entered the treatment room. The patient was sitting up on the stretcher smacking his lips. He looked to be 50, wearing tattered, dirty clothes. He was truly emaciated with no muscle mass and a tongue as thick as wood from dehydration. As I approached him, I heard the impatience in my voice when I sighed and said,

"Hello. My name is Dr. Davis. How can I help you?" I got no response.

He simply stared forward and twisted the bedsheet. After my several attempts, he startled me by yelling, "Don't bother me. I'm talking to the Lord, Jesus Christ."

His psychotic dialogue continued and contained a non-stop discon-nected series of references to the New Testament. Clearly, he was severely mentally ill.

I did a focused examination but was concerned that I could not examine him properly given that he was covered with filth from several sources. He was so disheveled that it was hard to peel off his clothes. Fortunately, the hospital had a tech who had worked there for many years named Frank. Before becoming an ER tech, he had played middle linebacker in a semipro football league. Then the injuries added up. He had the shoulders that every guy would love to have. Frank helped me strip the patient so that I could examine him. Other than encrusted personal waste, dried mud and some sores on his feet, he actually seemed physically OK except for being almost emaciated.

"Frank, I need a huge favor. Would you be kind enough to take this patient to the decontamination room and get him cleaned up?"

Frank looked at the patient, smiled at me, and said, "Sure, doc, but you're going to owe me." I had given him a bottle of red wine at Christmas and he was keen to remind me of my capacity for generosity.

Sometime later, Frank returned the patient to the treatment room dressed in hospital scrubs, slippers and a paper hat like those worn in the operating room.

I met him in the hall outside the room and asked, "How did it go, Frank?"

"Very easy. He was cooperative and easy to work with. An interesting thing happened though."

"Oh, like what?"

"Oh, like about the Bible and the Lord and Christ. I have always been a Southern Baptist and so we talked about God and life in general. He sounded like a highly educated person. In fact, he used some pretty big words."

With only modest attention, I said, "Hmm. Very interesting."

Shortly thereafter, I rejoined the patient and asked, "Do you feel better after the shower?" He looked at me with a vacant stare and said nothing.

"Frank tells me that you two talked about God and Jesus Christ. Perhaps you can tell me, who is the malefactor, Satan or Christ?"

Growling at me with obvious disdain, he said "If you mean the bad guy, obviously Satan."

Startled that he knew the word malefactor, I asked, "Are you indubitably sure?"

"Doctor, where did you go to college? Malefactor and indubitably are certainly pretentious and obscure words. So, let's try again."

I wondered, *how in the hell did he end up paranoid, broke and homeless?* This fact highlights some of the main difficulties ER docs have evaluating homeless patients with psychiatric problems. The patients are often unable to give you a believable history; they often have no medical records; whatever data can be retrieved is often unreliable; getting the history from the patient and other sources, if available at all, usually takes a long time—sometimes hours. While numbers vary from city to city, about 1/3 of the homeless in America are chronic schizophrenics. The problem has been made worse in recent years by the closure of state-operated in-patient mental health hospitals and too few outpatient mental health facilities. However, most patients who have suffered a lifetime of schizophrenia and are homeless have achieved only limited educations due to their disability and tend to not have the vocabulary this patient demonstrated. In contrast, some individuals who have schizophrenic-like symptoms, or who have been stable for years on medications, may suffer an acute psychotic break caused by a devastating emotional trauma such as the loss of a loved one or financial ruin or, more simply, running out of their medicines or deciding to not take them anymore. Their coping mechanisms are wiped out and they suffer a severe break with reality. While I am not a psychiatrist, it has been my impression that those with such an acute change in mental status are brought to psychiatric help in a timely manner by anxious family or friends. An educated man who is suffering from an acute psychotic break doesn't usually end up walking the streets in rags, unfed and unwashed. My experience over the years had taught me that while schizophrenics will often call God for rescue from Satan (me), usually they have been somewhat passive and not been aggressively hostile towards me. This man was. Honestly, I was stumped.

I tried again to get a history from him, but he drifted off into a psychotic never-never land. I asked, "Where are you from?" He gave me no answer. Do you have a family here in Virginia?" Again, he gave me no response but simply stared forward chomping on his lower lip. Pressed for time, I left him while I saw other patients.

His lab work came back and it was OK. I had sent a toxicology screen that was supposed to include blood and urine. He had refused to provide Frank with a urine specimen, so my toxicology inquiry was delayed. Psychiatric patients, once they are "cleared medically," are seen by the psychiatric social worker on call to determine if they need mental hospitalization. By this time, it was about 1 a.m. The social worker's name was Ruby and was a perfect fit for her job. She grew up in Georgia and had a wonderful way of using humor to get patients to confide in her. She was known to be able to fill the room with laughter and a positive attitude.

"Ruby, I need help." I described the patient as best I could, given his reluctance to speak to me.

After a few personal chuckles, she confided: "Dr. Davis, it's Saturday night and I've been besieged with calls from other ERs. I'm way behind. Would you please hold on to the patient until morning when my day crew comes on?"

The nurses fed the patient whatever food we could scrounge up at 3 a.m. Afterwards, he drifted off to sleep. At 8 a.m., I signed him out to the day shift ER physician, Kevin.

"This is a pretty interesting case. The patient was found wandering in the middle of the road at night and was brought in by a medic unit. Despite his psychotic symptoms and disheveled state, he seems highly educated. What's more, from time to time, he will answer my questions with a logical but hostile manner. He is OK medically although the 'tox' screen has been held up.

I spoke with Ruby last night and she said the social workday crew would see him this morning." I signed out the rest of the patients to Kevin and went home. As I left the ER, the day shift psychiatric social worker was due any minute.

At 8 p.m. I returned for my night shift. Right away the night shift charge nurse said to me, "Dr. Davis, Kevin from day shift has something interesting to tell you and wants you to call him."

My heart sank. When the doctor who had relieved you wants you to call him back right away, that is usually bad news. I was worried that I had screwed up and something awful had happened to one of the patients that I had discharged to home.

"Hey Kevin, this is Chris. What's up?"

"Chris, thanks for calling. Remember that guy who seemed like a crazy, homeless psychotic? You'll never guess what happened."

I was still not yet feeling good about this conversation.

"It turned out that three weeks ago, he was the state treasurer of a nearby state. Apparently, he was accused of being responsible for some irregularities in the management of the state's treasury. As his troubles mounted, his boss thought he was getting more and more off his rocker. Three weeks ago, he disappeared. Nobody could find him. His family has been frantically looking for him. His critics thought that his departure proved his guilt. This morning, Nancy Sullivan, the day shift psychiatric social worker, got the police involved. Nancy and the detectives figured it out. Apparently, there had been so many accusations against him with damning media coverage that he had a psychotic breakdown. He had been on psychotropic meds for years that no one had known about. Nancy was sure he had stopped taking them. After multiple phone calls, Nancy located his psychiatrist at home, and everything fell into place. Our psychiatrist on call cleared him for transport and so he went home by ambulance about 4 o'clock. Fascinating case."

More relieved than intrigued, I thanked him and hung up the phone.

On further reflection, I realized that I had been uneasy about how I had handled the case. What had I been confronted with? I was trying to take care of a hopeless, helpless, homeless, unwashed street person who seemed crazy. While I tried to hide it, I had been angry. Fed up. Another crazy, bad-smelling bum in my ER taking up my time that I knew I couldn't even begin to meet his needs. Why wouldn't he talk to me? It dawned on me that he wouldn't talk because he could see how pissed off I was. He perhaps was a bit crazy, but not THAT crazy. Frank, the friendly tech, had befriended him. They had talked about shared religious views that had given this patient respect and reassurance. Confidence. The patient did not trust me and now I could understand why.

Nobody likes unwashed homeless street people. In addition to the lack of hygiene, their enormous psychiatric and social needs make us in the ER feel totally unable to meet their fundamental needs. I asked myself, *was my demeanor in any way affected by his being a homeless vagrant or was some part of it due to his being full of hate for me?* I thought about that question carefully and decided that my disrespect was likely the cause of his angry reaction.

One of the constant challenges of being an effective ER doc is that, due to limited time, I had to "size up" a patient quickly. That has serious limits and forming an incorrect impression of a patient is a constant risk. Empathy takes time and may be inadequately rendered if the ER doc, swamped with other urgent problems at the time, picks up on the wrong clues. This patient had been rescued not by me with my ten years of graduate school education. The two rescuers were my good buddy Frank, whose kindness and empathy demonstrated the best way to communicate with this patient, and Nancy Sullivan, the social worker, who had been inquisitive when I had not been. She had the time and smarts to be a good detective.

Usually when an ER doc gets pissed off, it is because he/she has forgotten all of the hard-earned lessons they have learned about why it is important to not get pissed off! That certainly applied to me in this case. I felt badly about that. Too many frustrations, too much pressure on top of too much fatigue can shorten anybody's fuse. However, most experienced ER docs can tell when they are about to "lose it" and quickly apply the emotional brakes because they have learned that unmanaged anger is destructive to relationships. I learned early on that getting angry, especially at the ER staff, required me to spend a huge amount of time repairing the resulting damage. I made three changes in my behavior that I feel helped me.

First, I learned that treating fatigue with too much caffeine was often the match that ignited my fuse. Secondly, I learned that exercise helped me control my emotions. I was not alone in this discovery. Obese ER docs are very rare. Thirdly, and most importantly, I would come home and discuss what happened with my wife who is a brilliant internal medicine specialist. Her understanding, insight and advice taught me a great deal about why I reacted in the way I had and how to deflate my "Irish temper."

Leap Frog

In late June in 1994, while working my evening shift at Reston Hospital, summer fun turned tragic. At this stage in my career, after years of hard work, my family and I were enjoying the good life. I had a five-star marriage, financial security and finally, a generous vacation schedule. That night, I encountered two families like mine who had been happy and successful until tragedy changed both their lives forever.

Our exceptional nurses were managing an extremely busy ER that night. During my twelve-hour shift, I saw 43 patients—a personal record for me. I only remember one case.

Moving to pick up yet another chart, I heard the rescue squad radio blare, "Dr. Davis, this is Charley Dixon in Medic 24. We are transporting a 16-year-old male involved in a car crash. Except for a minor lip lac, he is basically unhurt. Unfortunately, the accident involved a fatality. Our patient seems OK. The fatality is being taken to Fairfax Hospital so as to not mingle the involved families. We'll be there in five minutes."

"Medic 24, I copy. We'll see you shortly." All of the nurses had heard the radio call and were psychologically prepared. They all assumed that our incoming patient had caused the crash but the paramedics were being discrete by not adding that fact over an unsecure radio. Their compassion for the family of the incoming driver was tempered by the need to be formal because a charge of vehicular manslaughter hung in the air.

The paramedics entered with the stretcher and, at the direction of the charge nurse, put the patient in the "trauma room." As I've described earlier, "room" is a misnomer; almost all of Reston's stretchers were separated only by those sliding yellow curtains that made privacy a constant issue. Like most modern ERs, this trauma stretcher was surrounded by the usual monitors, IV equipment, wall oxygen, wall suction and IV bags of Ringer's lactate ready to be started without delay. What differentiated this "trauma room" was that it was more spacious than average to accommodate the large staff sometimes needed to save the dying. Also, in order to provide maximum privacy, it was more isolated than the other stretcher areas.

As the paramedics quietly wheeled the stretcher into the ER, several features about the arrival of this "trauma" patient struck me as unusual. First, the paramedics were virtually silent as they arrived. Secondly, the patient lacked the medical accessories usually associated with a trauma patient: he had IV fluids running but no oxygen, no splints, no bandages. A slender, teenage male named Brad lay on the stretcher with his eyes closed.

When the nurses asked, "Brad, how do you feel?" he remained mute. This is a behavior that we have all seen in patients who are not being uncooperative but are simply blown away by the major tragedy that has suddenly enveloped them. Their psyche seems to close up like a box. They are terrified but emotionally numb.

The nurses proceeded to start the usual intake procedure for a new trauma patient such as vital signs, monitor, etc.

The paramedic, Charley, took me aside out of the earshot of the trauma area and described, "Doc, this is one of those cases that burns your heart. Brad, who is only 16 years old, was driving his dad's car with his girlfriend sitting beside him along with two other kids in the backseat. They were being followed by another vehicle driven by a classmate. They started playing leapfrog down a suburban road about ten miles from here."

"Leapfrog?" I asked.

"Yeah, this is a game that two drivers play where they pass the other's car. Once one vehicle successfully passes the lead car, the following car then tries to pass him. Well, Brad tried to pass the other car while rounding a blind curve. When he moved into the oncoming lane of traffic, Brad found himself driving into a head-on collision with an 18-wheeler coming toward him. The force of the crash pushed Brad's car back across the right lane and over a private fence. Amazingly, Brad was not injured. The kids in back and the girlfriend in front were taken to Fairfax Hospital. The two in the back seat were hurt but not critically. The girlfriend was DOA. The fire chief wanted to keep Brad separated from the parents of the girlfriend; he sent us a long way to get here."

I entered the treatment area and went over to evaluate Brad. "Brad, I am Dr. Davis. I am sincerely sorry to learn about what happened tonight." Brad said nothing but did everything I asked during the examination. "Brad, does this hurt?" Brad gave me a subtle, slow rotation of his neck whenever I touched, pushed, palpated, bent or rotated any and all of the parts of his body. Due to the high velocity of the accident, I was concerned about the possibility of a subtle but serious injury. The only problem I found was a small laceration to his upper lip, which was amazing given the forceful impact of the crash.

The charge nurse, Anne, was a pro I admired. About 50 years old, she spoke with a slow Southern drawl that I loved because she would never speak in the flash speed of medical staff from New York. I could understand her. In a tragedy such as this, the charge nurse is instrumental in managing other personnel to provide an optimal environment for the patient. Aware of the limited privacy afforded by the trauma stretcher area, Anne made sure that idle chit chat did not occur and that the nurses did not ask questions that might have legal implications.

I expected to find the parents in the family support room. Instead, I found them standing at the desk of the nurses' station. Dad was tall, with a slight belly and a white handlebar mustache. He was staring blankly off into space. His wife was sitting in a nearby chair and had her hands buried in her face as she recoiled from the reality she was facing. She took a deep breath and asked, "Doctor, what should we do for Brad?" As her tears flowed, the helplessness in her voice touched me. Her sympathetic question suggested that these parents would not scold Brad—not now at least. I offered, "Don't ask any questions now. Just reassure him that you love him, and you are all in this together. A soft hug always helps." She left the desk and went to Brad's side. Unfortunately, at this moment, two Fairfax County police officers showed up. They took dad to the family support room to discuss the case.

Anne set up the suture kit that I needed to repair Brad's lacerated lip. Mom stood next to the stretcher, reassuring Brad to an uncomfortable extreme. When I injected a small amount of local anesthetic, she would exalt, "Oh Brad. Dr. Davis is doing a beautiful job. You will be happy with the result." When I cleaned the wound, she would gush, "Oh Brad, you are so lucky. Dr. Davis is making this wound look new." When I would place a stitch, she would insist, "Oh Brad, you are lucky to have such an expert taking care of you." Throughout the process, Brad said nothing. When I was finished sewing the laceration, Brad rolled over on the stretcher and buried his face in his pillow.

After his interview with the police, Brad's father was clearly shaken. When Brad's mother returned from cheerleading my wound repair, the two withdrew to the hall, hugged each other and sobbed. I was tied up with other patients and did not have a chance to say goodbye to the family.

About a year later, I learned from Anne that the parents of the girlfriend who died had filed suit against Brad's family for an astronomical sum. How frightened and helpless Brad's parents must have felt. Anne believed that they settled for the full amount of Brad's family's available insurance: one million dollars.

I have been interested in the current educational efforts being made to educate teenagers about sex and drugs. To be sure, these are two areas fraught with peril for young people. But what about driving a car? Sure, teenagers may understand that one can turn right on a red light. Shouldn't they also be required to understand the basic physics about driving a car? For example, a car going 40 mph crashes with four times the energy as a car going 20 mph.

As Dr. James Forrest Calland, a trauma surgeon at the University of Virginia, says in his YouTube videos, *"The scariest time of being a parent is when your child is learning to drive."* His talk is brief and lists the five most common causes of teen car crashes. They include the following: being an inexperienced driver, driving with other teenagers in the car, driving at night, not wearing a seatbelt and distracted driving. In many states, each of these is illegal for inexperienced teen drivers. However, like most traffic infractions, the drivers are rarely caught by the police who are too busy. Telling such a teenager that such violations are illegal will not suffice.

I met a visionary police officer in Virginia who had a great idea. Whenever requested by a group of parents, he would take a small collection of 15-year-olds about to learn to drive on a tour of the jail cells. I tagged along once and enjoyed watching the stunned look on the faces of the kids he brought. He made a point of subtly jangling the keys to the cells. The kids who were all friends exchanged horrified glances. Maybe one of those could be saved from being another Brad.

Moving on:
The Pacific Northwest

Transition to Seattle

As I mentioned earlier, my wife and I graduated from college in 1968 and were married the summer after my first year of medical school. As I was making my way through my residencies and my years as an attending physician, Kathleen pursued an equally challenging career. After being part of a research team at Harvard and then the NIH, she decided to go to medical school too. She completed her training in internal medicine at GW, worked there for eight years and then joined a private practice of women internists in Silver Spring, Maryland. By 1985, we had two lovely children and had become fairly good at balancing the time commitments of family life and two medical careers. However, by 1995, we had lived in the D.C. area for 27 years and were ready for a change.

That summer, Kathleen and I took the kids on a vacation to the Pacific Northwest and loved all of the parks, trees, hikes, mountains and boating opportunities. After a few phone calls, I was quickly offered a job. We moved to the Seattle area the following year and have been delighted with that decision ever since.

I joined a nationally recognized emergency medicine group headquartered in Seattle. I was selected to be the medical director of the ER for one of their contract hospitals; these were two busy urban hospitals, both in Tacoma just south of Seattle.

After five years running ERs, the burden of administrative responsibilities made me yearn for full-time direct contact with patients. I had discovered that managing a busy ER department was a politically sensitive role and was better suited to a proactive extroverted personality. That wasn't me. Secondly, an ER director has huge responsibilities but no authority. Doctors and patients complained to me incessantly about genuine issues that I had no power to control or improve.

I needed a change. I decided to return to spending all my time seeing patients. I had a very high opinion of the ER docs in my emergency medicine group and decided to remain with the group and the same hospitals. Although I was very happy to be treating patients again, many of the problems that I struggled with as a medical director continued to remain unsolved. The major challenge then was that the hospital did not have enough beds to accommodate all of the ER patients who needed hospitalization. The net effect was that every night, we had patients in the receiving hallway who should have been in a hospital bed or, frequently, in an ICU bed. My energy and talents as an ER doc were tested every day. The following four cases from my Pacific Northwest practice remain indelible in my memory.

Dedicated Doctor

In late 1998, while working at a rural hospital in Eastern Washington, I got to know an unusually conscientious primary care physician, Dr. Matt Collins. He enjoyed a wonderful reputation with his patients and the entire hospital staff. He would round on his patients at 6:30 in the morning before going to the office, then return at 5:30 p.m. to revisit his patients. After rounds, he would come to the ER and just sit around chatting. When the ER was quiet, I enjoyed participating in the chit-chat with Matt. I liked him and we were becoming good friends. By 8:30 p.m. or so, the nurses would chide him to go home to his family. When he finally left, he'd wave to the nurses with a warm smile on his face. One evening, the hospital charge nurse was visiting the ER and had a discussion with the nurses about why Matt spent so many hours in the hospital when he had only six patients in the hospitalized. Naturally, this conversation led to speculation that he must be having trouble at home with his family. This was a small town where gossip has wings.

One Saturday afternoon the weather was gorgeous. The ER had only a few patients. Suddenly, we heard an enormously loud blast outside the ambulance entrance; it felt like the sound waves shook the whole ER. The nurses and I ran out to see what had happened. An old pickup truck sat right in the middle of the ambulance driveway. We rushed over and looked inside. The driver had placed the barrel of a shotgun into his mouth and pulled the trigger; he'd blown his head to smithereens. Every part of his head above his chin was a tangled bloody mess.

While I held what remained of his head in a towel, the staff placed him on a stretcher and moved to the trauma room. To identify the body, the ER charge nurse checked his wallet for some identification. The name on the wallet was Joshua Collins—Matt Collins' son.

Upon hearing this, I promptly sat down. This tragedy was too close to home. All of the empathy in the world would not assuage the terrible emotional pain about to hit unsuspecting Matt. I had the responsibility to call him—but I couldn't do it. I knew I didn't have enough control over my own emotions to be able to communicate directly with Matt. After a few calls, the hospital medical director placed the call. I do not know what was said, but Matt did not come down to the ER.

Over the next few days, rumors continued to dribble out. The Collins family had been going through a period of immense discord over the fact that Joshua had a learning disability. With his self-esteem in the trash, Joshua had started to use drugs. The family strife had continued to escalate.

Matt was known to be a cordial, non-confrontational man; he had great difficulty handling the stress at home. So how did he react? He avoided the anguish of his home life by almost exclusively dedicating himself to his job. This behavior is not uncommon. Physicians who are struggling with family or other personal problems sometimes, as a coping mechanism, hide themselves in their work. Such a doctor can create a persona of exemplary dedication. Everybody loves him—except his family. If his neglected wife files for divorce, many of their friends feel sorry for him and not her. After all, who can blame a doctor for being too dedicated?

Joshua certainly was angry with his father and he chose to punish his dad in the most devastating way possible. The details of Joshua's suffering no doubt were complex but unknown to me. Part of the problem, I suspect, was that Joshua wanted the same loving concern from his dad that Matt so generously rendered to his patients.

Hip Dislocation

During a quiet ER evening in Tacoma, the ambulance radio went off, "Dr. Davis, this is Medic 5. We are en route to your location with a 29-year-old female who reports that she dislocated her right hip while having intimate relations with her boyfriend. Apparently, this has happened before. She is not asking for pain medicine at this time. Her right thigh is flexed and internally rotated. The blood supply to her leg is OK and she has normal feeling in her right foot. Her vital signs are fine. We will be there in 10 minutes."

As the Medic 5 rescue unit wheeled into the ER, I could see that the patient's right thigh was flexed and pointed towards her left knee. This is the classical presentation of a patient whose thigh bone has been pushed posteriorly and has jumped out of the hip socket.

The paramedics moved her to our ER stretcher with great care; sudden movement caused her pain. Once she was on the stretcher, the nurses and I rolled her slightly to her left side and put pads under her right hip. That seemed to help the pain.

"Good evening, I'm Dr. Davis. You seem to be having quite a problem here."

In spite of her compromised situation, the patient was cordial and pleasant. She was slightly overweight; her hair was disheveled and she was wearing a Seahawks sweatshirt and a pair of denim blue jeans much too large for her. She was in pain but not to the excruciating level that I had expected.

"Oh Dr. Davis, I'm Madelyn Cooper. This is so embarrassing. About five years ago, I was in a car crash that wasn't my fault. This idiot ran a red light. I slammed on my brakes, but I still plowed into the side of his car. Because I had forgotten to put on my seat belt, my right knee slammed into the dashboard dislocating my right hip. The damage to my hip joint was bad and so I had to have a hip replacement. The other driver's insurance covered my hip replacement and enough cash that I decided not to sue. All was fine for about three years. But about two years ago, my hip popped out of joint while me and Nick...he's my boyfriend...were making love. Since then, it has happened about three times, every time only when we were having sex." She pointed to a tall, heavy set man standing a few feet away. "Come here darlin', I want you to meet Dr. Davis. Dr. Davis, this is Nick. He's my honey."

When Nick and I shook hands, I felt his vise-like grip. He looked to be 40 years old, 250 pounds and wore a worn-out brown leather jacket, denim jeans and faded leather boots. He seemed shy but spoke to me with a twang that conjured up the Deep South. His worried look towards Madelyn told me that he really loved her and was feeling terrible about what had happened.

Looking at Ms. Cooper's position on the stretcher, I wondered, "Ms. Cooper, judging from your current position, it seems to me that your hip has popped out in the backward direction. Have you ever had it push out the other way, towards the front?"

"No," she replied. That was very good news. Anterior dislocations are fortunately rare and do a great deal of damage to the hip joint.

I directed the conversation to what seemed like an obvious question. "Ms. Cooper, have you ever returned to see your orthopedic surgeon to have this corrected?"

"Dr. Davis, it's like this. I went to see an orthopedic doctor after the first time it happened. He saw me in the ER, put it back in place and thought that I would need repeat hip surgery. He gave me his card and I promised to see him in his office. I didn't see him again because I could not afford to. I am a hairdresser. As I am an independent contractor, I have no benefits, including no health insurance. While the insurance company did give me some cash, it was not enough for more medical care."

Madelyn studied my reaction to this story. "Dr. Davis, don't look so worried!"

Although I was worried, I needed to get that hip back in place without delay. The x-ray showed a posterior dislocation of the hip that matched her leg's position as expected. After looking at the x-ray, we agreed that I would put the hip back in its socket right away.

The enormous pair of coveralls Madelyn was wearing were obviously Nick's. As she had had no clothes on at the time of the accident, Nick helped her wriggle a pair of his monster overalls to cover her legs. I explained to Madelyn that I needed to visualize the injured area to make sure that there was no evidence of a huge bruise that would indicate bleeding around the injury. She closed her eyes and clenched her teeth bracing for the pain that was bound to occur. One of the nurses helped me pull the denim down over the hip area and I saw no sign of bleeding on the surface or deeper.

I went over the relocation of the hip with Madelyn. Having been through this a few times, she took the plan in stride. I asked her if she wanted any pain medication first. She said, "No thanks. I haven't needed it before." I admired her courage.

Nick asked, "Dr. Davis, can I watch?"

I glanced at Madelyn and she nodded her approval. "Sure Nick. Putting a hip back in place requires two anyway."

As we got underway, I thought to myself that this is one of the strangest damn maneuvers any ER doc has to do.

"Now Nick, I want you to put one hand on each side of her pelvis. When I tell you to do so, I want you to push down while I pull up her leg towards the ceiling."

First, I lowered the stainless-steel rails on each side and climbed up onto the stretcher wedging my feet against the inside of the rails. I immediately crouched down because, for a moment, it felt like I was going to fall off. Remaining in my crouched position, I had Madelyn's lower right leg between my legs. I told Nick, "OK, I am going to place both my hands around her right leg just below her right knee and then I am going to pull straight up towards the ceiling. Your job is to keep her flat on the stretcher while I pull."

"Got it," replied Nick.

Needing a way to keep her lower leg immobile, I positioned her lower right leg between my legs and against that ridge of my pelvic bone called the greater trochanter. Imagine a racing bicycle with one of those tiny saddles. The rider sits on the saddle using his greater trochanters. I used my trochanter bone as a fulcrum. By this time, I had an audience of two nurses, the x-ray tech and the evening shift nursing supervisor, all watching with rapt fascination. I placed both my hands around her right leg just below her knee, straightened her leg to the centerline and started to gradually pull up towards the ceiling. The thought again occurred to me that if one of my feet slipped off the stretcher rail, I would go crashing to the floor, which would have not done her right leg any good. I pulled a little harder but then noticed her butt was coming slightly off the stretcher. "Nick, push down harder." I pulled a little harder and harder still and, then, I heard a soft muffled "clunk." Her hip was back in place.

A post-reduction x-ray showed the hip to be positioned correctly. Madelyn was happy. Nick was happy. I was relieved. The nurses couldn't believe what they had just witnessed.

My suggestions to Madelyn to see an orthopedist fell on deaf ears. She was a nice person whose ability to walk would degrade soon. A half an hour later, with her instructions in hand, Madelyn sat up, grabbed her walkers and was ready to go. I thought that admitting her to the hospital would be a wise idea, but Madelyn refused. No insurance. Hoping for the best, I gave Madelyn the business card of the orthopedist on call. One of the nurses provided her with brochures on how to apply for Medicaid and the contact information to reach a social worker. We had done our best. Ultimately, Madelyn was in charge.

Nick approached me, and in a soft voice, asked, "Dr. Davis, I don't understand what I can do to prevent this from happening again." Good question. Thinking like a former mechanical engineering student, I was baffled as to what forces might interact during the manner of coitus he described that would cause such a dislocation. We both needed to check Google.

"Nick, I'm not sure. However, if she doesn't follow up with an orthopedic surgeon, I'm afraid it will get worse. It might worsen to the point that any more sex is out of the question."

Nick solemnly nodded, thanked me, and re-joined Madelyn to help her get underway. Nick clearly loved her a great deal and was profoundly worried about hurting her ever again. She was brave and not melodramatic. With Nick on her left and slowly using her walker, she hobbled out of the ER. The overalls of Nick's that she was wearing made it look like she was walking inside a denim tent. I liked them both and sincerely hoped that all this would eventually be resolved.

As I watched them leave the ER, I was filled with sadness and frustration at the unfairness of Madelyn's situation. This case is a perfect example of how a medical condition is exacerbated or unable to be treated properly because of the lack of affordable health insurance in America. Few things are as disheartening to an ER doc as recommending effective treatment for a patient only to know that such treatment is unaffordable to the uninsured patient. While well insured patients get deep discounts thanks to their coverage, those who are uninsured because they can't afford it or whose insurance covers a lot less than they realized, get crushing bills. Why do we have a system whereby the health insurance is provided by the employer? It goes back to WW II. Then a national wage freeze was in place while the war-time economy adjusted. Companies could not compete with other companies for workers by offering higher wages. Therefore, offering health insurance to potential new workers was a powerful lure. But look at what happens to their health insurance when workers are laid off or their company goes bankrupt? An equal problem arises when the CEO wants to show profit growth to the stock holders. Buying less expensive, and less comprehensive, health insurance for the workers is a good place to start. No other developed country in the world has such an outdated, fragile health insurance system. Health insurance in many such countries is considered a right and is provided by their government, paid by taxes. It is like Medicare without an age limit. Other countries offer insurance through private options also, but there is universal coverage. In our country, the most common cause of personal bankruptcy is medical bills. Once I visited an ER in St. Petersburg, Florida, to get an inexpensive antibiotic for a rash on my neck. For some reason, I didn't have my insurance card with me and was registered as "uninsured." I was seen by a PA, given the prescription and was out in ten minutes. My bill was $3,000! Unequal access to healthcare is, to my mind, the most unfair feature of life in the United States.

Heroic Rescue

During the autumn of 2005, I had been an ER doc for over 30 years and was wondering when it would be time to retire. Since I still loved my work, I began looking for a more sedate ER. In addition to continuing to work in Tacoma, a part-time ER position opened up in a small Washington State town known as Port Townsend.

Port Townsend is a seaport situated along the Straits of Juan de Fuca on the Olympic Peninsula northwest of Seattle across Puget Sound. I was attracted not only to this ER job but also to this town with its surrounding area of enormously tall evergreen trees and spectacular mountains. I thought of all the sailing, hiking and climbing activities to which my family and I would have easy access. The buildings in downtown Port Townsend were mostly built of old brick with stone placards with construction dates of 1906 or 1921. The charm of this main street's ambiance of days gone by felt comfortable and welcoming.

The hospital in Port Townsend was small with approximately 25 beds. The ER consisted of six beds surrounded by curtains. Not surprisingly, each bed had the same equipment that was typical of ERs thirty years earlier. That made me feel vulnerable because I had come to rely on high tech equipment found in a modern ER. Each shift had two nurses who were usually long-time residents of the town. Mature and polite, they treated me with warmth and kindness. Because the ER wasn't very busy, I had the chance to chat with patients. What a wonderful—and new—experience that was for me.

One evening in October, the weather was crisp, cool, slightly windy but with clear skies. For a few moments while on shift, I walked outside to enjoy the sight of the night sky decorated with hundreds of bright stars. In contrast to Seattle, I could see the stars almost all the way down to the horizon. As I walked back into the ER, I heard the speaker of the ambulance calling in.

"Dr. Davis, this is Hugh on Medic 1. We are coming in with lights and siren, as we have a lady with an amazing abdominal wound. She had obesity/bariatric abdominal surgery two weeks ago. Tonight, she coughed and ripped open her surgical site. She has exposed bowel. We have her abdomen covered with a sterile dressing, IV Ringer's running and we should be there in five minutes. Oh, she weighs 400 pounds! The fire engine company is coming with us so that we have enough lifting power to put her on a stretcher."

As her vital signs were OK and they were due shortly, I offered no further orders. Minutes later, I heard the ambulance brakes squeak to a stop followed immediately by the loud diesel roar of the fire engine and its screech as it also rolled to a stop.

I walked out of the ER to watch the unloading of this patient. There were eight firefighters and paramedics who were carefully and gingerly carrying the stretcher. With much effort, they pulled the stretcher up a short cement grade into the ER.

Hugh, the paramedic, exclaimed, "Doctor Davis, this is one for the books. The patient is a 45-year-old registered nurse who underwent bariatric surgery at the University of Washington Hospital two weeks ago. She lives here and has been home for the past week. This evening, she had a coughing spell. Her cough was so violent and painful that she lifted her dress and saw that her abdomen had ripped open through the surgical incision. Except for hypertension and type 2 diabetes, she is in adequate health. Her BP is 110/60, her heart rate is 120 and her glucose is 130. When I cut open her dress, I saw that her entire abdominal contents were exposed. Lots of small bowel but amazingly, not much bleeding. I covered her abdomen with a sterile drape for transportation here. She has IV Ringer's lactate running through her right arm and has shown no sign of serious bleeding. She works as an RN in a local clinic. She lives alone with her Labrador retriever. Knowing that she was going to the hospital, she was so alarmed about the welfare of her dog that the engine company promised to take the dog back to the fire house until things could get straightened out."

I thanked the paramedic for his report and walked over to talk with the patient. The nurses had already drawn the relevant bloods and sent them to the lab, started another IV, placed her on oxygen and attached the cardiac monitor. Her name was Barbara Hardy and she greeted me with a soft smile and the countenance of a patient who expected to die: calm, polite and peaceful. The sterile drape was still across her abdomen and showed only a few blotches of bright red blood.

"Ms. Hardy, my name is Dr. Chris Davis. I am very sorry that you are having such a terrible night and I welcome the opportunity to help."

She reached over and gently grabbed my hand. "Dr. Davis, am I going to die?" Recognizing the fact that she was an RN, I knew that empty reassurances would not help her.

"Ms. Hardy, the paramedics have told me that you have very little bleeding and your vital signs are off to a good start. Tell me, what happened?"

"As you can imagine, I have had a terrible struggle with my weight my whole life. When I reached 400 pounds, my internist and I decided that it was time to do something more aggressive. I underwent gastric bypass surgery at the University of Washington two weeks ago. Anyway, I did well after surgery and went home after several days. Tonight, while watching the Seahawks get pounded by the Cowboys, I had a coughing spell. I coughed and coughed. Then I both felt and heard my whole abdominal surgical incision tear open. Because I had the gastric bypass surgery, my incision goes from just below my ribs almost down to my navel. The pain was terrific, but not as bad I would have expected. I lifted my dress and thought I saw my small bowel creeping out of my abdomen. Holding my belly, I figured that I had better lie down quickly so that the bowel did not fall out. I shuffled over to the sofa, collapsed and called 911. Then she gently asked, "Dr. Davis, am I going to die?"

I was touched by her calm equanimity. I patted her hand and replied, "Ms. Hardy, you and I are in this together. But we must act quickly."

Doing a quick physical exam, I listened to her heart and her lungs while she remained supine. I then donned a sterile yellow gown, put on a face mask and sterile gloves. Using a sterile clamp, I lifted the dressing that the paramedics had applied and looked inside her abdomen. Her abdominal wound had been torn open in the centerline from just below her ribs down to her belly button. There was a small amount of blood leaking from the skin incision. A mound of small bowel seemed to want to creep into my hands, but it was not contracting in a serial fashion as you would expect a normal bowel to do. When a bowel stops doing its job of digesting, it is called an ileus. Fear, pain and trauma can cause an ileus. Though motionless, her bowel was becoming distended like an inflated tire. It was filled with gas. I worried that this enlargement of the bowel would cause it to extrude out of the wound. To reduce the gas, I asked the nurses to place a tube through her nose down to her stomach and, using gentle suction, the tube would pump out the stomach and hopefully deplete some of the gas.

I turned to one of the nurses and said, "Nancy, please take a sterile sheet, moisten it with saline under sterile conditions and give it to me to lay over her abdomen." Though this was an unusual request, she brought it to me, and I placed it over the patient's abdomen.

At that moment, anxiety raced through me. My brain yelled at me, *Good God, Chris, you are totally out of your depth! There is no way that you and this tiny hospital can save her.* Even though I was wearing a surgical face mask, I noticed that Ms. Hardy was closely studying my expression as only a nurse can do. Aware of her apprehensive looks, I turned to her and said, "Almost no bleeding. The small bowel is now protected with a sterile dressing. Next, I need to work the phones to get you back to UW to correct this."

"Dr. Davis, am I going to die?"

I patted her hand and said, "I sincerely and honestly don't think so."

The fire chief, paramedic and I met in a corner of the ER out of earshot from the patient. The paramedic said, "Driving her in an ambulance from here to the University of Washington Medical Center in Seattle would take about four hours depending on the ferries. We all know that the roads for such a trip are pretty chewed up with bumps and potholes. I don't think she would make it."

The fire chief agreed but then asked, "What about Life Flight?" Life Flight is a helicopter rescue force well recognized in Washington State for its excellence.

I responded, "Chief, that would be great. In the meantime, I will call the UW ER to let them know what has happened." I asked the fire chief to call Life Flight; experience had taught me that fire chiefs in Washington State are immensely respected by all rescue services. I called the ER at UW and was pleased that they answered after only one ring. As UW did not have an emergency medicine residency at the time, one of the medicine residents took my call.

"Hello, this is Dr. Davis at Port Townsend. We have a patient of yours who had gastric bypass bariatric surgery at UW two weeks ago. Tonight, she coughed, tore open her entire abdominal wound and is in danger of eviscerating her small bowel. We need to send her your way STAT." I gave him more details about the case, but then I got the impression that he wasn't listening.

"Has your general surgeon seen her?"

"No," I snapped. "That is not relevant. This is a small rural hospital and this lady needs advanced surgical care promptly."

"I'm sorry, Dr. Davis, but before I can accept her as a transfer, I have to get the OK from the bariatric surgery team and they are all in the OR now. They will call you back as soon as they can." It was obvious to me that this medical resident was very new to the ER and did not understand the difference between an elective versus an emergency transfer.

"Accept her?" I yelled. "For God's sake, this is your UW patient! Cut the bullshit because she is on her way. Have your bariatric team call when they feel so inclined!" I replaced the phone with more force than was polite.

I suddenly realized that I was reacting with the characteristic anger that I'd seen many frightened men display. I had just blown my top at this medical resident who was obviously new to the ER. My brain hollered at me, *Chris, do you understand what just happened? You were furious with this poor medical resident because you are scared. Now get your shit together and act like a grown-up.* I felt very embarrassed. I should have known better.

Nancy, the nurse, picked up the phone and started dialing. She looked at me, smiled and explained, "Dr. Davis, I am just calling the UW ER back to give them our phone number."

A few minutes later, Nancy said, "Dr. Davis, the UW ER attending is on the phone for you." Having embarrassed myself already with the UW ER staff, I scrambled back to respectability by adopting the deferential demeanor of a British diplomat. Immediately, the attending ER doc fully understood the mess I was in and we both agreed what to do next...helicopter transport.

The fire chief approached me glumly. "Doc, we've got a problem. Life Flight cannot take her. At 400 pounds, the patient exceeds the lifting power of all of their helicopters. The patient needs a stronger helicopter."

"Chief," I asked, "could the National Guard help us?" He was unsure.

Then, I had a brainstorm. As an Air Force flight surgeon in Iceland, I had flown several medical evacuation missions in helicopters to rescue Icelandic citizens. Those helicopters could lift thousands of pounds. Why couldn't the military provide that sort of help for American civilians? I knew that the military was the only resource that could save Ms. Hardy. So, I called the ER at the Madigan Army Hospital at Fort Lewis in Tacoma. The ER transferred me to the desk of the captain who controlled the Army's rescue service for Washington State. I had never heard of such a service.

Much as I loved the Air Force, anyone who has ever served in the flying portion of the Air Force will tell you the same story. The people are terrific, the missions are rewarding, but the bureaucracy is appalling. The old saying was that no USAF plane could leave the ground until the weight of the paperwork exceeded the take-off weight of the plane. I was concerned that the layers and layers of authorization that would be required to send a rescue helicopter for Ms. Hardy would take too long. She would die in the back of an ambulance making a bouncy four-hour trip to Seattle.

I spoke briefly to the Army captain at Fort Lewis, located south of Seattle, and explained the story. He asked a few questions and then asked to speak to my fire chief. I went about other tasks and did not hear their discussion. In a few minutes, the chief was smiling and speaking enthusiastically to the captain. The chief put down the phone and came over to me beaming.

"Doc, the Army is going to dispatch one of their medevac helicopters and will lift off in 10 minutes." We talked at length about the weight of the helicopter and where it could land. The chief continued, "Some military choppers are so heavy that they can sink in soft asphalt, so I am taking my team to the elementary school for landing. There is lots of space and the parking lot is strong enough for the helicopter to land. Gotta go, Doc!" With a cheerful wave of his hand, he departed while he began briefing his crews as to what they needed to do.

Relieved, I went to tell Ms. Hardy what we had arranged. "Ms. Hardy, the Army is sending a special helicopter to take you to Seattle where a fire department ambulance will take you from the helicopter to the ER at UW."

Immediately I speed-dialed the Lord to say, *Thanks. I will send you a more substantial prayer of thanks as soon as I get a moment.*

Ms. Hardy smiled as both eyes moistened up. "Dr. Davis, from the moment we met, I knew that with you in charge, I was going to make it. Thank you."

While I was not there, the fire trucks lined up on either side of the elementary school parking lot and outlined the landing site with their rotating red roof lights. Wearing night vision goggles, the helicopter crew had no problem landing. In the ER, I stopped to listen to the low-pitched *thwop, thwop* of the huge military helicopter as it passed over the hospital. Such a beautiful sound.

The helicopter took her to Boeing Field in Seattle. From there, an ambulance took her to the ER at the University of Washington.

While I never heard anything back from UW, one of the ER nurses told me weeks later that Ms. Hardy was home again and doing well—comforted by her Labrador.

I recall a favorite saying by an orthopedic surgeon earlier in my career. His case involved a lady in her 60s with liver failure who had taken a fall and had fractured her hip. The medical staff taking care of the patient felt that she was too sick to survive the needed operation. The orthopedist recommended surgery so that the patient would be able to walk again. I thought his decision was a gutsy call. As he readied himself to go to the OR, he smiled and said something to me that helped me throughout my ER career,

"Somebody has to have broad shoulders in this business."

That Army captain and the Port Townsend fire chief both had broad shoulders.

The Painful Shoulder

Jogging for me has always been a wonderful way to feel well and drain away accumulated tensions and concerns. During one afternoon jog, I stopped to rest on a park bench. Not far away, I noticed a young mother playing with, caring for and supervising four young children. I was amused to think that her superb situational awareness would have made her a great ER doc. But something else occurred to me. She was not only situationally aware, she was vigilant. Vigilant. I watched her rescue her kids from injury several times in a few minutes; her actions crystallized in my mind that vigilance is at the heart of situational awareness.

One Friday evening, I was working in a satellite ER in Tacoma; it was overwhelmed by the usual Friday evening crush. I was then employed by the biggest health maintenance organization in Washington State. This HMO had strategically placed large clinics that included ERs in and around Seattle. These were fully equipped ERs that routinely cared for patients who had life-threatening conditions and were fully staffed by experienced emergency medicine physicians and nurses.

Their Tacoma ER was modern, recently built and well equipped. It included two beds for critically ill patients. These two beds were on platforms and surrounded with the gear it takes to bail a patient out of life-threatening trouble. The three nurses working that evening were terrific. But that evening, I saw something that worried me.

As I've described previously, the triage nurses would place colored tape on the top of each chart to signal the level of urgency: green for not sick, yellow for moderately sick and red tape for patients who appeared quite ill. They would then place these charts in an ascending rack in the ER for everyone to see. My worry was that the triage nurse that evening was a new hire. I had no idea as to her experience, training and judgment. In addition, this rack of incoming patients was placed in a far corner of the ER where it was almost out of sight. I had kept a sharp eye on this triage rack. I had noticed that there were five yellow tagged charts of patients waiting to be seen.

I was only two hours into my shift and was feeling sharp, energetic and ready for action when I checked out the chart rack of waiting patients and saw that the triage nurse had put a red taped chart in sixth place. Alarm bells in my head immediately started ringing. The fact that she put this chart last in the queue validated my concern that she was inexperienced in routine emergency room work. To her credit, she had already brought the patient back to a room and instructed her to get undressed and into a hospital gown.

Her blood pressure was 110/60, while her heart was beating at 140 beats per minute. When a patient has lost a great deal of the body's fluids, either from bleeding or water loss from vomiting or diarrhea, the body has a preservation mechanism to buy some time. The blood vessels clamp down, thereby shunting the available blood to the brain and heart to keep those vital organs functioning. The heart rate picks up to keep the dwindling supply of blood or fluids racing through the body. The top number of the blood pressure is the systolic blood pressure. A fast heart rate with a normal systolic blood pressure means that the body is doing a good job of compensating. However, when the systolic blood pressure starts to fall, the patient is in shock and in great risk of dying.

When I entered the treatment room, the patient, Alecia Stevens, a slender woman of about 25, was sitting on the stretcher holding herself upright by leaning on her arms. She was sobbing and grinding her teeth. Her hair was disheveled, and she was in too much pain to talk. Fortunately, her parents were with her and the mother provided the story.

Fighting back her tears of concern for her daughter, she said, "Alecia, has been healthy all of her life, but this afternoon she suddenly developed abdominal pain. At first, the pain was in her lower abdomen but became progressively worse. At first, I thought…"

Seeing that the patient was in agony and not ready to answer questions, I interrupted the mother to ask, "Do you think that she might be pregnant?"

The mother quickly glanced at her husband. Clearly, this was a sensitive family subject and she was reluctant to disclose specific information. In one study, 80 per cent of young women in the ER with abdominal pain who denied being pregnant actually were.

"Actually, we think that she is," she replied cautiously.

As I approached this sobbing young woman, she cried out, "Doctor, please give me something for this pain!"

"Ms. Stevens, I want to help. Would you please lie down for me so I can check your abdomen?"

She glared at me with obvious anger that I was asking her to do something that she knew would hurt. Supporting her back, I gently helped her lie backwards. Before she fully lay down, she blasted a full volume, high pitched scream and immediately sat up.

"Doctor, I can't do that!"

"What happened?"

"Lying back is killing my shoulder!"

"Which shoulder?"

"My left!"

That did it. I knew then that she had free blood floating around in her abdomen. The most likely explanation was that she had a ruptured ectopic pregnancy. The relationship to blood in the abdomen and pain in the left shoulder is a classic in the annals of medical diagnoses. Free blood in the abdomen is incredibly irritating to the walls that surround the abdomen. When a patient with a significant amount of blood in the abdominal cavity lies down, the blood sloshes its way upward towards the diaphragm. The free blood in the abdomen irritates the left side of the diaphragm, which then sends pain signals to the brain. The brain, however, is not accustomed to receiving pain signals from the diaphragm. The theory is that the diaphragm's nerve pain fibers enter the spinal cord near the same point as do the pain fibers from the shoulder. So, pain originating in the diaphragm is mistakenly attributed by the brain as coming from the left shoulder. This causes such agonizing pain that the patient cannot or will not lie down.

I rushed back to the nurse's station and called out, "We have a ruptured ectopic in room 4. All hands-on deck. Please move her immediately to the critical care area."

Fortunately, two paramedics had just dropped off a new patient and were getting ready to return to their station. Exceptionally well trained, they immediately joined in to help. As the gurney rattled down the hall to the critical care area, every tiny bump in the linoleum made Elizabeth's pain worse. Once in the critical care area, the nurses and paramedics were quickly putting in two IVs to give her replacement fluids to raise her systolic blood pressure.

"Pulse 140, systolic BP 88," called out a nurse.

"OK, she is in shock. Please start 2 IVs of normal saline and run wide open."

Alecia's loss of blood made it difficult to start the IVs. The nurse finally placed two and the fluid ran quickly.

With acute blood loss, obviously the first priority is to stop the bleeding and transfuse the patient. As mentioned before, the Ringer's Lactate that we were putting into her was the same salt solution that comprises most of the body's fluids. For every pint of blood lost, it takes three pints of Ringer's to replace it. This is because normal saline gradually drifts out of the blood vessels into the surrounding tissues. However, for an emergency stop-gap measure, it helps.

"Please call the hospital as I need to speak to the ob/gyn right now."

Her mother pleaded, "Doctor, please tell us what is happening."

"I believe that she is bleeding inside her abdomen. We need to send her promptly to Tacoma General Hospital for surgery. She is in real trouble and we must move quickly."

Fortunately, the paramedics were then loading their gear and already to take her.

"But why is she bleeding?" demanded her mother as she squeezed my arm.

"While I am not 100 per cent sure yet, the most common cause of this in young women is a ruptured ectopic pregnancy."

"What is that?"

"Usually, when a woman becomes pregnant, her fertilized egg gradually travels down a special tube called the Fallopian tube and nestles into the lining of the uterus. However, if there is a partial blockage in the Fallopian tube, the fertilized egg get can stuck and start to grow there. After a certain period of time, the growing egg gets so large that it ruptures the tube. That can cause severe bleeding and only an operation can correct the problem. Her shoulder pain convinced me that she is suffering from bleeding in her abdomen."

"Well, can't you do a pregnancy test to find out first?"

I gently touched her shoulder and said, "There isn't time."

As she was visibly shaking, her husband sat her down on a chair. As they huddled together, I assumed they were praying.

A nurse approached me and said, "Dr. Davis, Dr. Blanchard is on the phone for you. He's the ob/gyn on call tonight at Tacoma General." I had only met Dick Blanchard once before at a Christmas party. We both loved sailing and had talked incessantly about the sublime experience of sailing on Puget Sound.

"Dick, I have a 23-year-old with an ectopic. Horrendous pain, left shoulder pain, mom says 'possibly' pregnant. Systolic pressure 88 and dropping. Two lines IV saline running wide open. Fortunately, Medic 1 happened to be here, and they are loading her now."

Dick was instantly focused. "Wow. Please tell the paramedics I will meet them in the ER. I will alert the OR and anesthesia now."

"Dick," I continued, "Her systolic BP holding at 90. Pulse still 140. Six hundred ccs of Ringer's in five minutes." The nurses had placed inflatable cuffs around the IV bags of saline. By inflating the cuffs, the pressure on the bag was making the fluid flow faster.

Alecia's mom approached me and pleaded, "Dr. Davis, can't you give her something for pain? She's desperate. Why does she have such terrible pain?"

"I wish I could. However, anything I give her for pain will relax her blood vessels and cause a drop in her blood pressure. One of the many mysteries in medicine is that, for now, we have no idea why blood in the abdomen is so painful. However, this symptom of extreme shoulder pain helps doctors to recognize the problem and start care right away."

One of the paramedics joined us and said, "Doctor Davis, we are ready to go." He turned to the patient's mother and gently asked, "Would you like to ride with us in the ambulance? We have room for only one."

After glancing at her husband, she nodded and followed the paramedic. The Tacoma General Hospital, thank God, was less than ten minutes away. Later that evening, Dick Blanchard called me back.

"Hey Chris, I've got quite a story for you. I met your patient in the ER when the ambulance arrived. After examining her, I took her straight to the OR. No paperwork, no lab studies, not even a completed chart."

Dick spoke like a guy who had just avoided disaster. I could tell by the intonation in his voice that he was either physically exhausted, emotionally exhausted or both.

"I opened her up and…and I suctioned one-half gallon of blood from her abdomen!"

I was astounded. If the average human loses 40 per cent of his or her blood, they die. The average woman has nine pints of blood in her body. Forty per cent of nine pints is 3.6 pints. A half-gallon is four pints. For that amount of blood loss, she should have been dead.

"Good God, Dick, how is she doing now?"

"She is in the ICU. She is getting her fourth pint of blood now. Fortunately, the blood bank had two units of O-negative blood, which we gave her as fast as we could." Women can receive transfusions of O-negative blood directly without waiting for the slow process of doing a type and cross-match to insure compatibility of the donated blood with the patient. Women in their reproductive years should not receive O-positive transfusions, as that can cause problems with any subsequent pregnancy. O-negative blood is rare and a precious asset in a blood bank that can meet the needs of patients suffering acute blood loss. Dick explained that after Alecia had stabilized, she had received two more pints of blood that had been cross-matched.

"Oh, Dick. Congratulations! What a save. You will always remember this one."

"Chris, thanks to you too. Her blood loss should have been fatal. The super care that she received from you and your nurses gave me just enough time to save her." Without saying so, he was referring to the rapid flow of fluids that we had started in the ER and continued all the way to the OR table. Despite her loss of blood, the Ringer's Lactate kept her blood vessels open, thus permitting her brain and heart to receive enough blood flow to keep her alive for those precious extra 25 minutes or so before surgery.

We were both silent for several moments. Wanting to end the call on a note of levity, Dick asked, "Hey, fellow sailor, are you going to the Seattle Boat Show in January?"

I laughed and we hung up. One of the blessings of this case was that I was fully rested at the start of my shift. My cheetah-level speed in handling this case was the product of vigilance, experience and lots of unused energy. What sometimes happens to an ER doc is that towards the end of a grueling 12-hour shift such energy has been burned up. Exhaustion can slow down the brain and blunt any ability to make quick assessments and decisions. It is a well-known fact that the most common cause of traumatic deaths among ER docs is a car crash after having worked an exhausting night shift. Whenever I came home after a late evening or night shift, my wife and our two children made a concerted effort to keep the house quiet while I got caught up on my sleep. Sleep deprivation and vigilance don't go together. In very busy emergency departments, disaster often comes quickly and without warning. A rested ER doc can be more vigilant. Vigilance saves lives.

The next night, I was working in the ER again. The charge nurse approached me with a lady on her arm. I recognized her as Alecia's mother. Her eyes were still red, perhaps from hours of crying. She told me that she had come to the ER to thank me and the staff for helping to rescue her daughter. She gave me a gentle hug and then asked, "Is there any way that I could thank the donors of those four units of blood that saved my daughter's life?"

I thought for a minute and then told her, "Gosh, I'm sorry to say that I don't know how that sort of thing is arranged." I suggested that she call the blood bank at the hospital to learn more. With the determination in her eyes, I knew that she would do her best to find out who they were and to call to thank them.

In October of 2019, I was at a meeting with some staff of one of Seattle's blood banks. I am a Rotarian. The blood bank and the Rotary Clubs in the Seattle area have been working together for years to help recruit blood donors.

The moderator of the meeting commented, "The Christmas holiday season is our worst time of the year. The need for blood is huge, but donors don't like to donate over Christmas and New Year's. This happens every year." I told the assembled staff about the case of the ectopic pregnancy. To my surprise, there was a swell of enthusiasm among the managers of the blood bank. What impressed them was the keen desire of patients, or the loved ones of such patients, who have received a blood transfusion to thank the person who donated the blood. After subsequent meetings, the blood bank management team formulated a plan.

The blood bank team clearly believes that if the patients who receive a blood donation had some way to thank the person who donated the blood that would increase the appeal to potential donors. As I write this, the blood bank is developing a program whereby, with the permission of the donor, a sticker would be placed on each pint of donated blood. The recipient could remove the sticker, which would reveal a telephone number to the blood bank office and a special code number. The recipient could call the number and, by providing the code, receive the contact information to reach out and thank the donor. A clear precedent exists in the organ transplantation program. If a donor, such as a kidney donor agrees, his or her name and contact information is provided to the recipient of an organ transplantation. This idea is in development and seems to make a lot of sense to me. Who knows? It might one day become the national standard.

Teaching Emergency Medicine
in Africa and Asia

My wife Kathleen is a board-certified internist who taught primary care and hospital medicine for many years to medical residents in teaching hospitals. One evening in 2004, she approached me and explained, "I have been doing some research and have found a great opportunity to teach medicine in Uganda."

Kathleen had learned about a highly regarded nonprofit called Health Volunteers Overseas (HVO). For the past 30 years, HVO has been arranging opportunities for American and Canadian healthcare workers to travel to developing countries to help strengthen these less advanced health care systems. Working with a liaison in each country, volunteers could expect to teach, and consult with residents, medical students and nurses in the host country while they are involved in direct patient care.

As Kathleen began to elaborate on her idea of participating in HVO, within two minutes I asked, "Can I come too?" I had simply no idea what this would involve, but experience had taught me that I always had a great time when I tagged along with my wife. As usual with our foreign adventures, I left ALL of the details to Kathleen, but I was truly pumped up. Since I love to teach, the idea of teaching emergency medicine in resource-limited countries promised an opportunity to learn tropical medicine and to adapt the material to fit the cultural norms and resources of the country.

Even before we left the U.S., it dawned on me that in countries with lots of medical resources, doctors tend to care for patients who live into their 80s. Accordingly, they often treat people with slow, chronic conditions such as hypertension, heart disease, COPD, diabetes, dementia and the like. However, in poor countries where the life expectancy is often less than 50, not only are the illnesses different, but they tend to *kill quickly.* Malaria, dengue fever, cholera, HIV, tetanus and, of course, poisonous snake bites would all be new challenges for me. I had so much to learn before I could teach anything.

In January 2007, after our trips to Uganda in 2005 and Laos in 2006, we decided to attend the University of Liverpool's three-month intensive course in tropical medicine. The "Loo School," as it is jokingly known, enjoys enormous international respect as a superb place to learn to recognize and treat the amazing spectrum of nasty illnesses with which developing countries must struggle. We joined a class of 90 other participants from a variety of developing countries and we all bonded quickly. The course was grueling with four hours of lecture per day and countless hours in the lab studying the blood and poo of numerous insects, bacteria, parasites, worms and other causes of disease under the microscope. This rigorous methodology introduced us to a multitude of tropical diseases with which we were totally unfamiliar.

This orientation served us well when, subsequently, we made a trip to Cambodia in 2008. In Cambodia, we began by familiarizing ourselves with causes of disease in that country by going to the lab to study the most common infectious culprits under the microscope. Our lab work and thorough background in these specific tropical diseases gave us a head start with our preparations to work with the local doctors and medical residents.

The following stories describe details of our experiences in Uganda, Laos, and then after our Liverpool course, our trips to Cambodia in 2008 and Bhutan in 2009.

As I was to discover, many of the world's poorest, most disadvantaged people welcomed us with a warmth that was touching. In particular, what we were to learn about the Buddhist culture and values is an inspiring lesson for those Westerners obsessed with time management pressures and wealth accumulation.

Uganda

Our first overseas teaching assignment with HVO was at the enormous city hospital in Kampala, the capital of Uganda. Kampala turned out to be more modern than I expected with several skyscrapers and an active nightlife. Located close to Lake Victoria, Kampala is surrounded by a countryside renowned for its luxurious flora and fauna. Unfortunately, at this time in 2005, the poverty rate in Uganda was among the highest in East Africa. Agriculture provided most of the employment. There were few job opportunities for skilled labor.

On our first day, as we were walking to the city's main hospital, I noticed several small vans and pickup trucks in the parking lot all festooned with the name and logo of several other international organizations who had also come to Uganda to provide medical help.

Kathleen and I were initially startled by the sight of the hospital. Built of concrete and painted a soft red color, it was three floors tall and large enough to cover an entire city block. Once we had entered, our HVO Ugandan liaison took us to meet the medical team with whom we would be working. The team consisted of one clinical professor named Dr. John Muwanga and four medical residents. Dr. Muwanga already knew that we were coming from America to teach medical care; he was visibly delighted to meet us. He was slim and courteous. He spoke with perfect English, and his immaculate white coat suggested professorial formality. He introduced us to the rest of his team. They were residents and medical students at all levels of training and eager to learn. As the entire team spoke English and various Ugandan languages, they could translate what the indigenous patients were telling us.

Dr. Muwanga took us and his team to the "central ward" of the hospital where virtually all of the medical patients received their care. The surgical and obstetrical patients were cared for elsewhere. All of the general medical patients were treated in two adjacent rooms, according to sex. The scene left both of us stunned. The room was so enormous that it felt like an aircraft hangar where commercial airliners might be maintained. The entire hospital was built to take care of 1,000 patients. However, the central wards alone had over 1,600 patients! As you can imagine, all of the beds were occupied by patients, while the remaining 600 patients were lying on the hard linoleum floor wedged between those occupied beds. Fortunately, a gentle breeze through the enormous windows helped reduce the pungent waste odors of the poor, sick and dying. This Kampala hospital provided no food for the patients. Instead, family members kept vigil at their side to feed them, help them to the bathroom, provide blankets and pillows, watch their IVs and help the patients cope with fear and despair. The patients and their families exchanged gossip with their neighbors about which patient in their immediate area had what disease and who was about to die. What heartfelt devotion they extended to their dying relatives! Deep love amidst the deepest of poverty. Touched, I glanced at the floor and then looked away.

Our team had about thirty patients for whom our doctors were responsible. We moved slowly from patient to patient as Dr. Muwanga provided a very brief summary of each patient's condition. During one patient encounter, as the patient's family crowded around the bed, Dr. Muwanga flipped through the pages on his census clipboard. He looked around and startled us with his question, "Where is the patient 765? He is supposed to be in this bed."

An elderly lady replied somewhat enthusiastically, "Oh, he died last night. So, now my son is able to use a bed and not lie on the floor." Beds were quickly filled as soon as a deceased patient was removed.

"What did he die of?" I asked Dr. Muwanga.

Dr. Muwanga checked the clipboard and replied, "He had a very high fever. He was still being evaluated and so we never did get a definite diagnosis."

One of the grandmotherly members of a nearby patient spoke serviceable English and understood my question. She repeated the question to those around her. Nearby patients and visitors began to shout out their theories with comments such as:

"He must have died of malaria. Didn't you see his chills? His bed was shaking."

"No, he died of typhus."

"No, that's wrong. He died of syphilis. The Good Lord's revenge."

"That's crazy. He told me that he was dying of tuberculosis!"

Once the noise quieted down, I quietly asked, "Dr. Muwanga, what do you think killed him?"

He turned to me and, after a soft sigh, responded with a facial expression of despair and resignation. We walked a little further and then he responded in a very quiet voice suggesting that the answer was secret. "I assume that he died of malaria. Most of them do. The situation here is most unfortunate. Many of the people in Kampala live at home under bed nets at night. But then, if they develop an illness of any kind, they come to this hospital." Motioning towards the huge windows that enveloped the room, he continued, "Look at the windows. At night, the windows have no nets to keep the mosquitoes out." I was about to ask him how many patients contracted malaria while in the hospital. But I stopped short and kept my mouth shut. I wanted to be Dr. Muwanga's friend.

Dr. Muwanga was describing falciparum malaria—the big killer. Kathleen and I realized then that even though many of these patients might have effectively protected themselves from this murderous disease at night in their own home, just being hospitalized had potentially exposed them to malaria-infected mosquitos because of the lack of bed netting---or even window netting. The subtle way in which Dr. Muwanga reported the lack of window netting clearly suggested that the problem lay with the government's management of the hospital.

The cause of death of the missing patient piqued my interest. During a short break from the team's rounds, I walked down to the basement to where the lab was located. Navigating the shabby darkness, I scouted from room to room until I reached the hematology lab where the malaria blood smears were studied. I encountered the very busy hematology tech and asked, "Would it be possible for me to look at the blood smear of patient 765?" He smiled at me and it was clear that not many international doctors routinely came down to the lab with such a request. After rustling about the table for a few moments, he handed me a glass slide with a thin layer of blood on it.

"Here it is. You will be surprised by what you see."

Normally, when one looks at a malaria smear, you see a field of tiny red blood cells. Malaria looks like tiny black dots in a red blood cell. Each black dot represents a malarial parasite that has invaded that blood cell. Such stricken blood cells look like a set of miniature cherry tomatoes that have been lightly sprinkled with pepper. Normally, such a patient with malaria might have 2 to 5 per cent of his red blood cells showing the malaria parasite. That is enough to make the diagnosis. What I saw under the microscope amazed me.

"Good Lord," I said to the technician, "There are parasites all over the place!"

The technician appeared pleased to be visited by a doctor whom he could teach about malaria. He told me something I will never forget, "Yes, I did an actual count. Over 40 per cent of the red blood cells are infected. If you had seen the patient a few minutes ago, he would be dead before you can get back upstairs. You see, in Uganda, many patients have been exposed to malaria all of their lives. They have developed antibodies to malaria that protect them so they can tolerate mild exposures. However, when a patient with some immunity develops an overwhelming infection, even these partial defenses are not enough to protect him. In the blood smear of such a patient, like this fellow, you will see many more parasites than you would in the blood smear of a patient with no immunity." This resistance has been well described in the medical literature among African people. But I knew that I would not need to look it up. Kathleen would certainly know all about it.

After I returned upstairs to the central ward, our team visited several more patients that had been assigned to us. Dr. Muwanga did all of the talking. While I don't recall many specifics, the most common symptom complex appeared to be oscillating chills, fever, sweats and headache, all generally suggestive of malaria, tuberculosis or HIV. Symptoms included a cough lasting several weeks—tuberculosis? Chronic weight loss with intermittent diarrhea—gut parasites and or HIV? At this point, I realized how much this experience would teach me.

The team finished rounds at lunch time. Dr. Muwanga suggested that I visit the hospital's emergency department to see how I could be of help there.

Then Dr. Muwanga revealed the reality of his life as a staff doctor at Kampala's main hospital. Addressing Kathleen and me, he stated, "I and many of the senior doctors here leave the hospital at noon to take care of those additional responsibilities that have been assigned to us. Good day." With a smile and a handshake, he left. Hmm. I got it. One had to conclude that due to the poor state of the hospital, the staff of doctors would be poorly paid by the government. It did not take a detective to conclude that the staff physicians left the hospital in the afternoon to practice medicine in private offices in order to earn a living wage. Follow-up care at the hospital was obviously left to the residents.

Shortly after rounds were finished, I met one of the charge nurses. Very tall and thin, she looked like a potential collegiate basketball star. She spoke to me with a formal courtesy suggestive of a strict professional hierarchy. "Dr. Davis, in your country, how much anti-venom do you give to a four-year-old child bitten by a cobra? I have a child here who received a cobra bite last night. Her very upset parents carried the child all night to get to the hospital. Would you please take a look at her?"

Feeling both a sense of dread and an awareness of my clinical inexperience with snake bites, certainly including cobras, I approached the stretcher. The poor child showed no signs of life. She was not breathing, and I could not feel a pulse. I shined a bright light into her eyes. Her pupils didn't constrict which, as I've discussed in other cases, is indicative of a dead brain. Cobra toxin destroys the victim's nervous system. A person usually becomes paralyzed and can no longer breathe. Her skin was very cool. She had been dead for many hours. Interestingly, she had several small bruises, suggesting that she may have lost her ability to clot, which is a complication related to the venom of East African spitting cobras. Her parents were standing by the table exhausted and distraught. My sense was that the charge nurse brought me over to the family to reassure them that a white doctor from America had declared their child dead.

As both the nurse and the parents spoke Luganda, the nurse translated her conversation with the parents for me. Speaking directly to the parents, she started with, "We are very sorry, but your child is now in heaven. You did all that you could to save her. You are both very brave." She then put her arm around the shoulder of the mother who by this time had no tears left. Certainly, the charge nurse hoped that I would provide kind words for the parents. I bowed my head slightly to show respect and spoke the most empathetic words that I could find in my brain on such short notice. After the parents had left, I just stood there, transfixed by this image of a beautiful child murdered in her own home by one of nature's most surreptitious killers. A toxic brew of anger and anguish swirled through me. Quietly, I walked away from her body while I worked on getting my stunned emotions under control. Later the charge nurse repeated to me that her parents mentioned something about this being God's will. Really? I appreciate that such a belief could provide emotional solace to these poor devastated parents. But for me, it begged the question: Why would a loving God want to murder a little girl?

As I reflected on this thought of God's will, I realized once again that my childhood indoctrination in Catholic dogma and faith had been seriously challenged by my immersion in the science of biophysics at MIT. Although this mother's comment did not make sense to me, I remembered with affection something my own mother had said to me. As a flippant teenager skeptical of religion, I told her that there was no such thing as a miracle. She smiled and said softly, "The birth of a baby is a miracle." What a beautiful thought. Perhaps not everything is explainable.

After lunch, I spoke with Dr. Bucada, the administrator in charge of emergency care. After warmly welcoming me, he described the hospital's emergency department and how it operated. What posed as emergency care was the following set-up. A patient who comes in through the emergency entrance is first triaged by a nurse. If that nurse feels that the patient is sick enough to require a physician's evaluation, the patient is walked—or carried—up a flight of stairs to a mezzanine. On this mezzanine level, there are several beds occupied by patients. When I went there, I saw the patients lying on cots but no physicians. It turned out that the care was rendered by residents who also had to cycle back and forth from this emergency care area to the wards where hundreds of patients required attention. So, the residents would quickly come to the emergency mezzanine, see the patient and order a few tests and then would disappear to the main treatment area. The only job of the residents was to determine if the patient was sick enough to require admission to the hospital. If the patient was still sick after 24 hours, he was admitted. Such a patient then was absorbed into the chaos on the main floor. It was easy to understand why the residents were not interested in hearing me talk about emergency care; there wasn't any.

I turned to Dr. Bucada and explained, "I came from America to teach emergency medicine. What is the best way for me to do that here?"

He replied, "I'm delighted that you asked. The doctors here are all generalists. Most of them have no special interest in emergency medicine and we have no specific program for teaching the subject. Our greatest need is to train the nurses; they see the patient first. The nurses are the ones who need to determine if the patient is sick or not sick. Unfortunately, they have had no specialty training in emergency medicine either. Please start there." I was pleased that there actually was a need that I could address.

The next day, the administrator had arranged for the ER nurses to have two lectures a day, one early in the day for the morning and night shift and a second presentation of the same lecture in the afternoon for the evening shift. My wife, who is more skilled using computer software, helped me polish my PowerPoint slides. I had four more weeks to go before we were scheduled to move to another teaching hospital further south. Accordingly, I developed a course on emergency medicine, divided into 20 talks beginning with the basics.

To my delight, about 12 nurses showed up for the first lecture. Apparently, other department heads also sent some of their nurses to the lecture series. All of the nurses spoke English very well and were excited about my course. Initially, I started the lecture by asking leading questions expecting a reply. No one would answer any of my questions. I am sure that this Socratic Method had never been taught to them before and they were shy. So, I adjusted and began with the following summary:

"Patients who are carried in with trouble breathing or terrible chest pain will go quickly to the mezzanine to be seen by the residents. But what about all of the other patients who walk in needing help? Eighty per cent of the information you will need to diagnose what problem a patient is experiencing will come from the history—what the patient tells you. The key is not the pulse or blood pressure. It is not the x-ray or the labs. If asked appropriate questions, most of the time the patient will provide you with the information you need to determine what is causing their illness or injury. You, the nurses, are the first to see the patient and you have the earliest opportunity to understand the patient's problem. You start his or her healing process."

Upon hearing this, the nurses quickly exchanged glances, smiled and whipped out their notebooks. The beauty of this approach was that the nurses understood for the first time that they were actually key players in diagnosing the patients' problems, and maybe even saving their lives. They were excited.

My PowerPoint slides featured how to get started getting the history in an organized fashion. I taught them the American Heart Association method.

I began, "Ladies, getting a complete and accurate history from the patient is the first and most important step. A word that will help you remember what to ask the patient is the word, 'SAMPLE'.

'S' stands for signs and symptoms,

'A' stands for allergies,

'M' stands for medications taken by him or her,

'P' stands for previous medical problems,

'L' stands for last meal and

'E' stands for events preceding the illness.

In reality, it is sometimes better to ask about preceding events along with the signs and symptoms."

We discussed the details of each clue and then practiced the interview technique. One student would be the imaginary patient, while another nurse would practice an interview in front of the class. To be sure, many were terrified about being embarrassed. Keen to avoid that problem, I gave lots of help to the first few nurses. As their knowledge and confidence increased, they needed less and less help.

I gave brief PowerPoint lectures about the most common and deadly illnesses in Uganda. First, I used slides to illustrate and describe these lethal diseases such as malaria, HIV, pneumonia, abdominal conditions, wound infections and others. Next, I would turn off the PowerPoint to discuss how each of these conditions might present to the nurse. For example, I might start with pneumonia. After the slide show about pneumonia, I would then act as an imaginary patient and have the student, using the SAMPLE pneumonic, interview me. Later, I would have the imaginary patient be one of the nurses. The imaginary patient would be secretly assigned an illness by me and told to review the illness the night before so that her answers would be consistent with a person with that illness.

In the next lectures, I would focus on recognizing emergencies. For example,

Nurse: "What problem are you experiencing today?"

Patient: "Oh, I've got pain in my stomach."

Nurse: "When did it start?"

Patient: "Last night. It woke me up."

Nurse: "What is the pain like? Burning? Stabbing. Cramping?"

Then the nurse would ask the questions that help refine the possibilities such as, "Did you have nausea, shortness of breath, obstetrical problems…?" In my presentations, I focused on serious or life-threatening conditions such as pneumonia, malaria, heart attack, appendicitis, ectopic pregnancy and others.

The nurses' excitement, laughter and applause were reassuring to me. It appeared that each felt that she had the tools needed to provide an accurate appraisal of a new illness and to recognize potential life-threatening conditions. They felt needed. They felt important. Their sense of professional self-respect grew.

The charge nurse told my wife, Kathleen, that on the very first evening after the course, one of the nurses was able to quickly diagnose a case of appendicitis and called in the surgeon to whom she proudly described her findings. She credited my course for the patient's successful outcome.

Prior to our departure, at a noon time ceremony, the Minister of Health presented me with a certificate of appreciation and each of the nurses received a newly devised accreditation.

The great reward to be found in teaching medicine is that an instructor is able to leverage his/her knowledge to help a great number of healthcare professionals treat their patients. This Uganda teaching experience was a win-win; both the nurses and I as the instructor experienced appreciation and success. As my dear old dad used to say: "The greatest gift that a person can receive is the opportunity to perform meaningful work."

Laos

The practice of medicine differs depending on the cultural context in which it develops. Kathleen and I spent three months, from January through March 2006, in Laos teaching Western-style medicine to Laotian doctors and nurses. A friend of Kathleen's from Wisconsin, Dr. Rosemary Quirk (real name), was working at that time with her husband, a combined internist/pediatrician, Dr. John White (real name), in Laos. She invited us to join them. Our experiences on this trip provided a unique glimpse into Laotian attitudes regarding the Vietnam War and how their culture and beliefs impact their medical practice.

We were stationed at a hospital in Vientiane, the capital city. Vientiane is small by Southeast Asia standards. With a population of less than one million, its history dates back to the 16th century. Throughout our stay, we constantly saw reminders of this history in the architecture, sculptures and Buddhist ceremonies. Kathleen and I stayed in an apartment building with statuary, thick red carpets suggestive of British aristocracy and a tight cloister of manicured gardens surrounding the front entrance. As we walked down Vientiane's tree-lined streets, we encountered sculpture gardens, ornately decorated monasteries, wats (temples) and old French colonial buildings. Our apartment was very close to the Mekong River. I enjoyed jogging for miles on the verdant trails along the river. Each morning, Kathleen would attend a free outdoor yoga class along the edge of the Mekong. As the Laotian yoga teacher led the class, she stood on a platform with the sun rising exactly behind her; it cast a red and yellow glow on the awakening city. Several times a day, small processions of Buddhist monks in brilliant robes would pass under our apartment window on their way to prayer services or seeking alms.

As medical instructors, Kathleen and I were assigned to a private hospital outside of Vientiane, which had a relationship with Health Volunteers Overseas. The medical staff of Laotian physicians, residents and nurses was our student body. After hospital rounds each day, Drs. Quirk and White ran classes for the residents. There, guided by the residents' interests and requests, we taught how to manage both medical and traumatic emergencies. Medical equipment for training was in short supply, so we had to improvise. One day, Kathleen went to the local market where she bought a large side of raw pork ribs. Using this as a substitute rib cage, she taught the staff how to put in a chest tube to drain away harmful fluids trapped in the thorax. (Pretty cool for an internist.) In addition, I focused on cardiac emergencies and taught the American version of advanced cardiac support and intubation at a special three-day conference organized by Dr. Quirk, which was attended by 100 doctors from all over Laos.

Although Vientiane reflected its ancient history, it also offered surprisingly modern and diverse dining options. By this time, the Europeans had discovered Laos. At the end of each day, we dined out at a fabulous European or Asian restaurant. Vientiane reportedly hosted 22 restaurants featuring every type of European cuisine. Kathleen and I went out one evening to a lovely Italian restaurant. A bottle of wine, two dinners and dessert plus gratuity came to less than seven dollars.

One weekend, Kathleen and I chose to visit a beautiful rural village, Vang Vieng, three hours north of Vientiane. It was located high in the mountains a few hundred miles from the Cambodian border. As we arrived in Vang Vieng, the mountains dominated the landscape with tall, pointed summits suggestive of the Alps and were covered by countless green trees alight with the bright colors of their flowering blooms. We were squired about by a tall, thin Laotian teenage boy wearing a Chicago White Sox baseball cap who called himself Borum. He was enthusiastic to see us and asked us as many questions about the United States as he could squeeze in while being our guide. After a brief walk along a rice paddy, he took us into a shaded area with tall trees where the Hmong villagers worked. We saw 24 Laotian women surrounded by their children; these women were busy sewing backpacks, purses, blankets and hats that would be offered for sale to the tourists in Vientiane. As we strolled among these chatting, focused ladies, they each gave us a cheerful nod and went back to work. On the far side of the sewing area, swinging gently in the wind, was a multi-colored hammock. Hmm. How does one sew while lying in a hammock? Borum invited us to meet the hammock swinger. He was a slightly portly male who was the boss of the sewing circle! He greeted us with an indifferent nod, but never got out of the hammock to say hello. So much for gender equality in rural Laos.

Near where the ladies were sewing was a sheltered area that I assumed was to offer the ladies protection from the rain as well as a spiritual meeting place. While Borum was chatting, I noticed hanging from the entrance something that looked like the conical metal shade on a large reading lamp.

Pointing to the source of my curiosity, I asked, "Borum, what is that?"

As he laughed, he replied, "Oh, that thing. That's our village bell."

Mesmerized, I slowly walked over to inspect the "village bell." While my tour of duty with the Air Force did not start until after the Vietnam War was over, I had learned a great deal about the planes, bombs, bullets and jet engines of that era. Stopping a few feet from the "bell," my suspicions were confirmed. This was the nose cone from a USAF MK-83 general purpose, 1,000-pound bomb. (That's correct. A bomb full of half a ton of TNT was called by the Navy and the Air Force a "general purpose" bomb.)

Without prompting, Borum launched into an explanation about the village bell.

"Long before I was born, the American War came to Laos. My father used to tell me that big and fast fighter jets flew over us day and night. This bomb fell into that rice patty over there," he told us as he pointed to a water-soaked field. The bomb never exploded. So, the villagers took it apart and used the explosive powder as fertilizer. We kept the pointed end of the bomb and have used it as our village bell." Then, he chuckled and swept his right arm in a full arc over the village and said, "If the bomb had exploded, it would have blown away our whole village." That was a casual remark that I'll never forget. Borum did not realize that in countless unmarked locations in Europe and in Southeast Asia, unexploded bombs, mines and artillery shells lie hidden in the dirt and continue to be a daily threat to those who till the soil.

Towards the end of the Vietnam War, the North Vietnamese army attacked U.S. troops in Vietnam and then withdrew over the border into Cambodia. President Nixon made the controversial decision to disregard Cambodia's neutrality and ordered the bombing of the North Vietnamese troops while they sought sanctuary in adjacent Cambodia. The U.S. aircraft that had been carrying this bomb had been intending to drop it over Cambodia. I suspect that the pilot had made a navigational error. In the days before GPS, aircraft navigational errors were routine. Or, just as likely, that aircraft could have been damaged by gunfire and the pilot was just trying to keep it flying by jettisoning all extra weight. Whatever the cause, this "general purpose bomb" was one of many that had been dropped on unfortunate Laos with no intention or purpose.

As Borum led us away to return to Vientiane, I turned around to soak in the sharp, jagged mountain peaks surrounding Vang Vieng as they turned pink in the setting sun, illuminating a carpet of greenery in the valley below. My father, brother-in-law and my cousin's husband all bravely suffered in the Vietnam War. One died from lymphoma attributed to his exposure to Agent Orange. The Buddhists' belief in the importance of forgiveness has largely enabled Southeast Asians to forgive America for the War. I believe that many Americans have not forgiven themselves nor their country's leadership for the Vietnam War. Consider the irony that, 50 years after the deaths of more than 50,000 U.S. servicemen, communist Vietnam has become an honored trading partner for America.

Back in Vientiane, the medical staff of the hospital would hold meetings twice a week to discuss difficult and/or interesting cases. Kathleen and I sat in on these conferences where both Lao and English were spoken. These small conferences were instrumental in teaching us how the Laotian cultural beliefs impacted their medical practice. On one particular day, one of the medical residents described a case that featured a wide variety of acute neurological problems in a woman who had given birth a few days earlier.

In Laos, the postpartum care uses a protocol practiced in several Asian countries. Sadly, Laos in 2006 had both the highest maternal and child mortality in Southeast Asia. Most of the births occur at home and only about half of the expectant mothers receive any antenatal care. In a remarkable paper entitled "Perceptions and Understandings of Pregnancy, Antenatal Care and Postpartum Care among Rural Lao Women and their Families," the author and his associates described a postpartum ritual that amazed us. (Note: This paper was archived by the NIH.)

Quoting from the paper:

"A vital practice in many areas is giving birth on a 'hot bed', also known as 'mother roasting,' whereby mothers lie on a bamboo bed with hot coals underneath it after birth in order to restore the body's energy and close off the vaginal opening again. Based on a humoral system in which heat is thought to be lost during the 'open' state of delivery, the goal of the 'hot bed' and all postpartum care is to restore the mother to equilibrium by continued heating of her body.

"After the cutting of the cord, the baby is bathed and then placed on a bamboo bed near the mother. The mother is then prepared for the 'hot bed' by having water from a traditional healer blown on her and having tight black and red cotton tied around her wrists, ankles and neck in order to prevent bad spirits from entering her.

"With a fire lit beneath it, the 'hot bed' is thought to strengthen the woman's health and accelerate contraction of the uterus."[2]

During our session on the postpartum care of this patient, the presenting medical resident said, "On the third day after 'lying hot,' the patient developed multiple problems." His summary included numbness first in her right

---

2   Vanphanom Sychareun et al Perceptions and understanding of pregnancy, antenatal care and postpartum care among rural Lao women and their families. (http://creativecommons.org/licenses/by/4.0/)

hand and then on her left side. In addition, the new mother complained she had a diffuse headache, that her eyes did not seem to work together and that she felt confused.

Apparently, to the rest of the medical staff, this was a syndrome occasionally seen in women who were 'lying hot' shortly after childbirth. After a few polite questions had been asked, no physician in the conference offered an explanation for these symptoms.

When the resident finished his presentation, Kathleen and I looked at each other with amazed silence. After the meeting, Kathleen and I asked the medical resident if we could see the patient. The resident responded enthusiastically. "Most certainly. This case is most strange, and I would like your opinion."

Later that same day, that resident took us to a small hut about a block away, which functioned as a center for post-delivery care. This tiny structure was made with cinder blocks with a thatched roof and painted a dull gray. We ducked our heads as we entered, and I was just able to stand up. The room was painted a cheerful yellow. The shades were drawn covering all of the windows. Upon entering, Kathleen and I both felt uncomfortably warm. The room was small with space for only one cot. A light smoky haze irritated my eyes reminding me of my collegiate days trying to adjust to contact lenses. There, on a cot that was raised about three feet on cinder blocks, rested a slender Laotian woman. I was standing perhaps three feet away and I felt that the heat from the cot was already unpleasant. This new mother was indifferent to our arrival, showing us only a vague awareness that suggested she was either exhausted or perhaps had received some sort of sedation. The resident would not let me touch the cot. I simply could not imagine how anyone lying over a bed of hot coals with only brief breaks each hour could be happy or comfortable. To the left of the patient was a small crib; it was made of bamboo and held a sleeping child. There was no thermometer in the room and no way of measuring the temperature of the cot on which the new mother was lying.

The month was January and the winter, by Laotian standards, had been unusually cold. Looking about the room, trying to be subtle, I drifted over to one of the shaded windows near me. I pulled the brown shade slightly back and—to my horror—I saw that the window was closed. All the windows were closed!

I then asked the resident, "Why are these windows all closed?"

The resident replied, "It has been quite cold this month. Since we are trying to keep the new mothers warm, we have closed the windows so that the heat will not escape."

Now it all made sense. A woman lying for days on a smoldering fire with no ventilation in the room had developed a host of strange and variable neurological complaints. The scenario fit carbon dioxide poisoning perfectly.

Carbon monoxide poisoning is the world's most common cause of non-drug related accidental deaths. When a fire burns with an inadequate supply of air, the resultant smoke is full of carbon monoxide, which is invisible and odorless. The aerosolized poison can cause serious damage to the brain and its associated network of nerves. Such toxic injury often includes headache, vomiting, dizziness, confusion and variable neurological deficits such as numbness in the arms or legs, bleeding in the eyes, seizures and a host of other problems. Unfortunately, a patient with a moderate exposure to carbon monoxide may develop these symptoms quickly or may not develop them up to a week afterwards. When the symptoms develop several days after such an exposure, the patient, for example, may not recollect anything about the circumstances that resulted in the problem. While I worried about the mother's health, alarm bells rang in my head about the baby. Children are more susceptible to the toxic effects of carbon monoxide than adults; it can damage a baby's brain for life. Was this poor little tyke asleep in the crib having his brain progressively more injured every minute? I felt tempted to scoop up the baby and run outside to the fresh air. Unfortunately, doing so would ruin my opportunity to teach the medical staff about the dangers of carbon monoxide for the benefit of future patients.

Speaking to the resident, I asked, "With the windows closed and the fire burning in a closed room, aren't you concerned about carbon monoxide poisoning?" To my surprise, the resident had never heard of carbon monoxide poisoning!

Kathleen, the resident and I all left the hut together. Upon stepping outside, we were surrounded by the chilly air made moist by the nearby Mekong River. Yes, it was cold. It was certainly true that a newborn baby must be kept warm. Then it occurred to me. Delivering a baby at home in an inadequately warm environment could be fatal to an infant. Perhaps, that was the original logic behind the practice of "lying hot." I wondered if the desire of birth attendants to keep the baby warm had later become connected up with concerns about the mother's gynecological recovery.

There is a blood test called the carboxyhemoglobin test that can measure the amount of carbon monoxide in a patient's blood. Since a patient with carbon monoxide poisoning will commonly seek help for a host of weird symptoms, many healthcare providers forget to consider carbon monoxide poisoning and assume the problem is simply hypochondria. The delay in the appearance of some of the symptoms may prevent both the patient and the physician from putting carbon monoxide poisoning on the list of possible causes.

Later that same week, we attended the medical conference again that was led by the same medical resident who had taken us to see the patient "lying hot." I stood up and mentioned my concern about carbon monoxide exposure to the mother and baby. After I proffered my opinion, the resident blew up into a rage. He clearly felt that my question embarrassed him in the eyes of his colleagues for not considering the possibility of carbon monoxide. This was the only time in a Buddhist country when I witnessed a display of anger. I chose to not press the matter further, as I did not want to damage my welcome with the medical staff.

Over the years, I have reflected on this case many times. My sadness about that new mother and her baby sustaining possibly permanent neurological damage has never left me. Even worse, considering that the medical staff had no knowledge of carbon monoxide poisoning and no blood test to verify its presence, my warnings had received no credible consideration. Why did that happen? This reveals a tricky part about a Westerner teaching medicine in a country with its own unique culture. "Evil spirits" can be blamed for causing a patient's illness that otherwise cannot be easily explained. While the Laotian resident did not specifically blame "evil spirits" as the cause, my sense was that he did not need to do so. In Laotian medical practice, "evil spirits" appeared to be the default explanation for the unexplainable. A second possibility was that the tradition of "lying hot" had been so long standing through generations, even among the educated classes, that it was inconceivable to believe that it caused harm.

I now feel that I was too judgmental about physicians working with very limited medical resources in a poor country when they invoked spirituality to help explain a medical mystery. We Christians sometimes do that too. In modern American ERs, families devastated by the death of a loved one, as well as the Ugandan parents who lost their daughter from a snake bite, will sometimes try to submerge their grief with the explanation that their loss was "God's will." Laotians, like Americans, frequently will invoke a spiritual explanation for tragic events. Doing so can provide emotional rescue.

Cambodia

In February of 2008, Kathleen and I accepted another assignment with HVO to teach medicine in Cambodia. Our previous experiences in Laos and Uganda as well as our three-month course at the Liverpool School of Tropical Medicine the previous year helped us more feel comfortable with the challenges ahead.

One Monday morning, we joined the Cambodian medical doctors who were seeing their patients in the 15-bed medicine ward at the Prince Sihanouk Hospital of Hope. Its mission was to care for those who couldn't afford care elsewhere. The physicians were quite an impressive group. The Cambodian Head of Medicine, Dr. Kruy, (real name), who had joined us, impressed me as a true leader. The physicians had been trained by her and despite the heat, were all professionally dressed in white coats, white shirts and ties. Not only were they up to date on the status of their patients in the medical ward but they had clearly researched best care available in Cambodia for their patients' illnesses.

At the start of our rounds, Dr. Kruy introduced us, "Dr. Christopher Davis is a specialist in emergency medicine and is visiting from the United States. His wife, Dr. Kathleen Davis, is a specialist in internal medicine. They have come a long way to share how Western medicine might help us care for these very sick patients." The physicians gently bowed in our direction.

Before we got underway, I felt concerned that the material we could teach them referenced drugs and techniques with which they were not familiar. Recent advances in U.S. medicine prior to 2008 had been enormous, particularly in intensive care medicine. We had at our disposal dozens of different drugs for infections, heart disease, bleeding problems and a myriad of other illnesses. I felt a little embarrassed that we were expected to teach U.S. standards of medical care when these fine young people had far more limited resources, including laboratory tests and medications.

The ward in this Cambodian hospital was rickety with age. The patients in their stretchers were separated by sliding curtains, which provided an inadequate barrier against the transmission of infectious diseases. There was no wall mounted oxygen, defibrillation equipment and suction apparatus, all of which would have been the minimum for a U.S. ward. Since there were so few beds, patients had to be super sick to be admitted from the 200 or so patients seen in the outpatient clinic each day.

Our small group moved forward to approach the first bed, one of four in a row.

Bed #1. A small, undernourished male lay motionless on the stretcher. While I could see that he was breathing, he did not move or open his eyes as we spoke at the foot of his bed.

Dr. Kruy nodded to one of the junior physicians. He was clearly nervous as he reported, "This patient is a man about 40 years old. He was unconscious and unable to speak or move. He has a long history of drinking alcohol." He added that the patient was not known to have a family and had been addicted to alcohol since early in his life. This was one of multiple admissions for this patient who by now was well known to the staff.

I asked, "This man is clearly in a coma. Why do you think that has happened?"

The resident took a deep breath and replied, "We are unsure…uh, but think perhaps he has had a head injury…but, uh, but we found no blood in his hair and an x-ray of his head was normal." Clearly, this resident was concerned that I would criticize him for some clinical oversight.

I realized that this patient needed a CAT scan of his head. Alcoholics frequently fall and often sustain a head injury that causes bleeding in or around the brain. The hospital had no scan equipment, so I elected to avoid looking like another snobbish, condescending American medical professor. I rendered my three-minute canned dialogue about alcoholic brain damage and then we moved on the next patient in bed.

Bed #2. Dr. Kruy explained, "This patient came to our hospital three days ago with pneumococcal pneumonia. He was unconscious on arrival and has remained so."

I asked about his treatment so far. Here I saw an opportunity to teach. "What did his spinal tap show?"

One nervous resident was holding the chart. He looked at the floor as he spoke and shuffled his feet. He glanced repeatedly towards Dr. Kruy for some sign of approval as he responded, "His opening pressure was high. The spinal fluid had a cloudy color to it. Under the microscope, too many white blood cells were seen. The Gram stain showed lots and lots of gram-positive diplococci (Pneumococcus, a type of bacteria that commonly can cause serious brain infections in addition to pneumonia.) We treated him with very high doses of penicillin, but without improvement. We now think his brain had been too damaged to recover."

I nodded approval. Except for the use of an older antibiotic, I thought the care was spot on, especially considering the limited resources available to this young doctor. I commended him for his care, and we moved on.

Bed #3. We moved on to the next stretcher. This patient was also in a coma! The story was straightforward. He had been struck on the head with a club during a brawl. The x-ray showed a linear fracture along the right side of his head. The surgeons had opened his skull at the site of the blow and had drained out a large blood clot. No CAT scan, no EEG and no further neurological tools.

I asked the resident, "Are his pupils fixed and dilated?"

After having my question translated by Dr. Kruy, the resident replied, "No, both pupils are weakly responsive to light." While still in a coma, his pupillary responses indicated that he still had some brain functioning.

Wow. Three patients in a row, all in a deep coma! I made some superficial references about the pathophysiology of the cause of the coma in each case, but—so what? These doctors had done all they could with their resources. I had not come 8,000 miles to be the Ugly American.

Bed #4. Dr. Kruy presented the fourth and final case. This patient was a young man in his 20s named Arun Sok suffering from—you guessed it—coma. This poor fellow had falciparum malaria. Despite the aggressive administration of all of the medicines known to Western medicine, he failed to rally and had lost consciousness two days earlier.

Malaria was and is the major infectious killer in tropical climates. Some of the Anopheles mosquito species carry the malaria parasite. Interestingly, only the female mosquito bites humans and mostly at night, dusk to dawn. An infected mosquito carrying the malaria parasite bites her victim and draws out a small amount of blood. During this process, the mosquito introduces into the victim the malaria parasite that she is carrying. The parasite sets up shop in the patient's red blood cells and then reproduces rapidly. In about 48 hours, the infected red blood cell ruptures, dumping a tremendous number of freshly minted parasites into the patient's bloodstream. High fevers, drenching sweats and a variety of signs and symptoms caused by the spread of the parasites knocks a patient flat. The worst occurs when the parasites invade the brain. The resulting neurological damage can be severe or fatal.

While it is true that bed nets reduce the ability of the mosquito to attack the patient at night, the system is not 100 per cent effective. As we had witnessed in the Uganda hospital, this netting is not always used. Or when it is used sometimes, circumstances occur in which its protective barrier is breached. Perhaps a mother hears her child wailing in the middle of the night. Chances are that she will get out of bed to attend to her child and just hope for the best, knowing that her disturbance of the bed net may compromise its effectiveness.

Focusing once again on Bed #4, I asked Dr. Kruy, "What did this young man's blood smear and spinal tap show?"

"His blood smear had shown innumerable malaria parasites and his spinal tap looked almost as bad."

I went to the side of the bed. I called out his name, "Mr. Sok, can you hear me?" No response. Next, I tried to stir him to movement by performing a notoriously painful test on him. I placed a ball point pen over the fingernail of his right index finger and pressed. Hard. Then harder. No response. I took a flashlight and looked at his pupils. I could not convince myself of any response.

Dr. Kruy commented, "We have had no improvement using the best medicines available. These are the same medicines used in the United States, correct?"

I reviewed his list of medicines and agreed. Western medicine had nothing to offer beyond what had already been done.

"What are you going to do now?" I asked politely.

Dr. Kruy responded that they were going to try an herbal medicine developed by the Chinese. She understood that it had worked well in China for this kind of severe malaria. I tried to hide a condescending smile and thought to myself: *Herbal medicine for malaria parasites that had filled the brain leaving the patient virtually dead? Come on.*

I was becoming worried that our visit was not going to substantially help their desperately ill patients. The doctors were adequately educated but had nothing approaching the newest tests and therapies found in Seattle, Boston or Atlanta. I spoke a little bit about the pathophysiology of cerebral malaria, but interest in the topic had clearly waned. We parted and agreed to meet again tomorrow.

The next morning was gray and overcast. The overnight rain had bumped the humidity to a level reminding me of why I did not live in the tropics. Reluctantly, I put on my white coat feeling quite confident that the heat and humidity would quickly overwhelm my deodorant.

The team met and exchanged pleasantries. As my wife and I knew the cases, we proceeded down the line quickly.

Bed #1. Brain injury probably due to alcoholism. No change.

Bed #2: Pneumococcal meningitis. No change.

Bed #3: Head injury from a blow from an ax handle. Died during the night.

Bed #4: Cerebral malaria.

This last patient had received the Chinese "herbal medicine" during the previous evening. What we saw amazed us. He was intermittently rolling about in the bed and mumbling. His movements were not purposeful, and his brain was clearly severely injured, but my wife and I were quite startled to see such an improvement.

"Dr. Kruy, what was the medicine that you gave this patient? Some herbal medicine from China?"

Dr. Kruy clearly enjoyed seeing the look of surprise on our faces. "Ah yes, we gave him his first dose shortly after we finished rounds yesterday. He looks better, no?"

"What is the name of this medicine?"

"Artemisinin.' We have never used it before."

The next morning on rounds, my wife and I asked that we start at Bed #4. The patient appeared completely normal! His movements and his Cambodian speech seemed perfectly intact. I was so stunned I thought I needed to sit down.

Turning to Dr. Kruy, I exclaimed in a volume that must have startled her, "My God! He's awake! How did you do that?"

Dr. Kruy gave me what must have been the broadest grin of her life.

Using Dr. Kruy to translate, I asked the patient: "How do you feel?" In response to the question, the patient simply smiled, showing his multiple missing teeth, and shrugged his shoulders. After a few glances at Dr. Kruy for reassurance, the patient reported that he felt OK.

Dr. Kruy asked, "What do you remember of the past few days?"

The patient smiled again and shook his head. Further questioning by the staff of his name, age, home and all of the normal demographics indicated that his memory was almost normal.

To be completely honest, I had no previous firsthand knowledge of this medication. At the Loo School, multiple references were made to the drug, but I didn't appreciate its power. Considering how rare falciparum malaria cases are in the Unites States, the American medical establishment had not yet "locked on" to this new discovery whose proof of efficacy was coming from the developing world. As you can imagine, I scrambled to learn all that I could reviewing my medical databases. The story of this amazing medicine continues to fascinate me today. Artemisinin was discovered in wormwood and had been used in China as an herbal medicine for 2,000 years. Chinese scientists started the study of artemisinin as an antimalarial in 1967. Successfully introduced in multiple countries in 2001, it was so effective against the falciparum malaria that it was quickly credited with saving millions of lives around the world.

For many years, medications that were developed and rigorously tested using quality control in labs in Western countries would be accepted as having proven value. Sad to say, pharmaceutical companies in the United States and other developed countries are in a bind. They have to make a profit. Imagine the board of such a company having to choose whether to make another anti-depressant that the patient will probably need to take for years or to make an antibiotic that the patient will only take for two weeks. There has not been a new class of antibiotics developed in the developed world since 1987. However, now in the United States, there are 51 brand names antide-pressants on the market taken by about 16 million patients for long times for a total of more than $13 billion annually in revenue. Imagine a scientist trying to persuade a big pharmaceutical company to develop and market a Chinese medicine developed many hundreds of years ago that is derived from a plant. Assuming it actually worked, it would be useful in the United States for only about 2,000 cases per year where treatment lasts two weeks. So, I am not surprised that it took the United Stated so long to pay attention to artemisinin. In fairness to American pharmaceutical companies, their commercial success depends on following the money.

In 2005, the prestigious British medical journal *Lancet* hailed the drug as safe, effective and a "magic bullet" against malaria. However, it took four more years before its benefit had been conclusively demonstrated in the developed world. The Swedish pharmaceutical company Novartis developed the drug in a form to meet Western standards. However, Novartis did not seek FDA approval for use in the United States because the company felt few Americans ever contracted the disease and it cost $1 million to simply file an application to the FDA! When Kathleen and I were in Cambodia, the FDA was starting to evaluate artemisinin. By 2009, the FDA approved artemisinin hailing it as among the most effective and safe malaria medications ever discovered. As of this writing in 2020, a form of artemisinin is available from

Amazon at 20 cents per day, claiming it fixes a myriad of problems. This is unfortunate because used alone it causes artemisinin resistance in malaria patients, which can severely limit treatment options.

My first-hand experience witnessing the effectiveness of artemisinin has helped me realize that Western medicine could use a dose of humility. Now, thanks to this amazing "herbal medicine," we can save many more lives of those afflicted by this mosquito-borne killer.

I wonder how many more "herbal" medicines are awaiting discovery. This story reminds me of one of my favorite aphorisms, "Your brain is like a parachute. It doesn't work if it won't open."

Bhutan

By 2009, I was ever steadily creaking towards retirement. Kathleen suggested one more overseas trip—this time to Bhutan. The HVO management team had told us that the Bhutanese medical leadership was keenly interested in educating its doctors about emergency medicine. Since they did not have a teaching program in emergency medicine, this trip would be a logical fit for me.

At this time, Kathleen and I were living in the Seattle area. We loved being surrounded by evergreen forests and tall, snow covered mountains. What a pleasant surprise Bhutan turned out to be. Bhutan is a small country surrounded by Tibet to the north and Nepal and India to the south. When we arrived in the capital of Thimphu, the enormous evergreen trees covered Himalayan mountains reminding us vividly of the beauty of Washington State.

Bhutan's government is a Buddhist theocracy and the entire culture of the country is focused on living according to the values of the Buddhist faith and preserving its culture and traditions. In the capital city of Thimphu, for example, all of the adult government workers were required to wear traditional Bhutanese clothing while at work. When not working on the weekend, these same people would be fine with wearing denim jeans.

In addition, all laws enacted in Bhutan must comply with the standard of equitable economic and social development while also conserving the natural environment.

While we were there, this humanistic value system was supported by the economic security that Bhutan enjoyed at the time because of the massive amount of hydroelectric power it generates from the many Himalayan Mountain rivers that course through the country. Most of this electricity is sold to India which supports about one quarter of Bhutan's budget expenditures. However, as Bhutan has no sea ports, it has proven difficult to grow its economy.

The ER in Thimphu's national hospital was small and quiet. Eight patients lay on stretchers aligned along the walls; many were often surrounded by the patient's family. When I first arrived, I saw nurses but there was no doctor. When the working ER doctor returned, he was surprised to see me, as he had no idea I was coming. Over the next few hours, I learned the details of how their ER operated. The small size and limited available resources meant that the "turnaround time" for labs and x-ray was long. The electrical system in the hospital was weak to the point that when an x-ray was taken at night, the electrical drain dimmed all of the lights in the hospital. This lethargic support system in the hospital enabled the ER doc to leave the department for extended periods before coming back to check on his patients. He exhibited a relaxed patience such as I have never seen before.

Over the next few days, I met and worked with several of the Bhutanese physicians. When I explained that I was there to teach emergency medicine, many were disappointed at first. They had hoped that I had come only to take on shifts to make their life easier. However, as I consulted on several cases the first week, the physicians realized that I was an experienced ER doc who had come to teach them how to do a better job. It was like turning on a light switch. Suddenly, I was deluged with questions about ER diagnoses and care. I felt relieved.

We had to make several adjustments while we settled into our lives in Bhutan. We had arrived in February and it was quite chilly; the temperature was in the low forties with no central heating in the apartment buildings. We learned to adjust by moving portable radiators around and by eating and studying in our parkas. Although we were aware of the Buddhist tradition that prohibits the killing of living things if at all avoidable, our first night was startling. Thimphu was overrun by homeless dogs, hundreds of them. A chorus of them barked and howled through the entire night. We had a squad of five or six dogs, led by the biggest dog on the block, living right under our bedroom window; they partied all night. We were sleepless for the first few nights until we got the hang of it. Since there was no animal control program while we were there, I was not surprised to learn that rabies and tick-borne illnesses were common. In recent years, the rabies problem has improved thanks to implementation of the vaccine.

Several of the patients I was asked to consult were tourists who had not taken the usual precautions about drinking the water. Abdominal pain and diarrhea were common. Even experienced travelers did not understand that mosquitoes in Thimphu carry dengue. In contrast to mosquitoes that carry malaria, dengue mosquitoes fly and attack during the day. Diarrhea and headache were common sequelae. Those tourists with serious problems such as needing major surgery had to be airlifted to Thailand for specific care.

Part of my plan was to make every ER doc on the staff qualified to run cardiac arrests properly. Due to staffing schedules, I ended up meeting with each of the doctors individually. We would review EKGs, CPR and appropriate drug therapy. Since Bhutan had no medical school, all of the doctors had been trained in foreign countries such as India, Sri Lanka, Thailand and even Cuba. Surprisingly, there seemed to be a wide variety in the quality of education each doctor had received. The graduates from Sri Lanka's internationally respected medical school at the University of Colombo were well read, focused and knowledgeable. Graduates from India were variable. I was stunned when the only graduate I met from a Cuban medical school had not the faintest idea how to read an EKG.

Prior to our arrival, high-level, highly paid foreign consultants had evaluated the hospital processes. Upon their departure, they provided the government of Bhutan with complex and highly technical recommendations that were impractical in this setting and unaffordable. As we were only staying in Bhutan for one month, I wondered what cost-effective improvement to patient care I could make that would last long after I had returned home.

The problem that bothered me the most was that the time required for a patient to be seen, evaluated and treated in this Bhutanese hospital was glacially slow. To speed up this process, I put up a white board with slots with every patient's initials, what their problem was, what labs and x-rays were pending and all of the other data points that the ER staff needed to know where in the process each patient stood. At a glance. I wanted to replicate the patient-status board in the ER at the George Washington University Hospital that I had found to be so useful many years earlier. The doctors were at first skeptical; they probably thought this suggestion was just a case of a know-it-all American telling them how to run their operation. But the nurses loved it and encouraged the doctors to adopt it. When I left Bhutan one month later, the board was running smoothly and the operation of the ER was, I was told, much more efficient.

Throughout my visits to Southeast Asia, I became fascinated by the degree to which Buddhism reached into the hearts and minds of true believers to give them a sense of peace, security and serenity. I will always remember a medical conference that my wife and I attended while in Bhutan. The speaker was an infectious disease expert from the Washington University in St. Louis who spoke about how the excessive use of antibiotics can create problems. While antibiotics can usually help manage an infectious disease, used indiscriminately, they can also knock off the friendly bacteria which we rely on for our body's health. At the end of the talk, the Bhutanese Director of Medicine for the hospital pointed out that it was not in the Buddhist value system to indiscriminately kill organisms that are of no harm. In other words, killing off friendly bacteria was against a central tenet of the Buddhist religion.

As I mentioned, I did not see nearly as many extremely ill patients in Bhutan as I had seen in other Asian countries because so many were sent to Thailand. Without doubt, the biggest challenge that I found was the variable level of medical education and training among the physicians. This deficiency may have been the core of the HVO's interest in sending volunteers like me to teach.

Our visit to Bhutan was unique. Living in a culture focused on enhancing everyone's life was certainly a new experience for me. Bhutan has become an international icon of the Buddhist religion's value system. I think their model of focusing on individual happiness through supporting health, education, culture and the environment, has worthwhile lessons worldwide.

My Last and Favorite Story

Shinagawa

The incoming call from the rescue squad on that quiet summer evening in 1995 resonated through the entire ED; the voice of the paramedic had the "pressured speech" of a man under stress. I dropped what I was doing and went to the radio.

"Medic 5, This is Dr. Davis."

"Dr. Davis, this is Brandon on Medic 5 inbound with what I think is fulminant pulmonary edema. The patient is a 68-year-old male with a long history of congestive heart failure…" Brandon went on to quickly describe a patient who was extremely short of breath and sounded to me like he was in extremis.

Brandon told me that his ambulance would arrive in less than five minutes—not much time. I turned from the radio and spoke to the nurse, "Marcia, please set up for intubation. Anne, please call the respiratory therapist STAT." Actually, my orders were unnecessary, as these marvelous nurses knew exactly what this patient was going to need.

When the ambulance crew rolled into the ER minutes later, their patient, an elderly, obese white male, looked critically ill and had a terrified look in his eyes. Despite high oxygen flow through his mask, he was sitting bolt upright on the stretcher, struggling to breathe and soaked in sweat. He was so short of breath that he was able to talk to me only one word at a time. George Martin was his name.

The nurses placed Mr. Martin on a "code bed", which was surrounded by the equipment necessary to rescue a patient who was in great danger of dying. I began my exam by checking the vital signs the nurses obtained: blood pressure 160/100—too high for a sick heart; pulse 130 beats a minute—too fast for a sick heart; respiratory rate 40—much too fast for a tired heart. When I listened to his chest, his lungs sounded like the loud bubbles a child makes with a straw by blowing into a bottle of water. His heart had a rapid to and fro sloshing sound that reminded me of our washing machine at home. His legs were swollen, soft and spongy. The patient was dying from pulmonary edema. (You might recall that his presentation was identical to that of Mr. Bayles who presented to the ER at Boston City Hospital when I was a volunteer fifty years earlier.)

The explanation of pulmonary edema is simple—but successful treatment is not. As we saw with the case of Mark Mateo in "Doctor, No", patients with weak heart muscles, or previous heart attacks, are not able to pump blood efficiently through the heart and out to the arteries of the body. The nurses and I immediately started our most aggressive treatment protocol as practiced at the time: IV, high flow oxygen, a diuretic to help Mr. Martin pee out some of the extra fluid, nitroglycerine and multiple small doses of morphine; all of these helped to reduce the workload of the heart. His oxygen level was low, but adequate for the moment so I decided to hold off putting in the endotracheal tube. He seemed to slowly be getting better. His EKG revealed evidence of old damage but nothing suggestive of a new heart attack.

After about an hour of intensive therapy, he was breathing more slowly and appeared less frightened. I glanced at the bag collecting urine from his catheter and was pleased to see he was peeing briskly, which served to rid his body of extra fluid. I reviewed the blood tests and, so far, had not found any disastrous numbers.

I took his wife aside to learn what had happened.

"Oh doctor, I feel terrible. We drove over the weekend to see our grandchildren, but George had forgotten his medicine. He takes a lot of medicine because his heart is so weak." Such a common story.

I continued to get the extra background history on George while his wife and I stood a few feet away from his stretcher.

"Where does he get his medical care?" I asked.

"He goes to the Naval Hospital in Bethesda. He always loved the Navy, but suffered greatly during WW II." As my Dad had spent 36 years on active duty with the Navy so I could immediately dial in to her sense of pride and loyalty to the service.

I approached George's stretcher and rested my hand on his shoulder to reassure him. Still sitting up in the stretcher, George was now breathing well enough to speak to me in short sentences. We ran through the usual questions about chest pain, nausea and other symptoms that go along with another heart attack. He answered "No" to all of these questions.

"Mr. Martin, your wife tells me that you are a Navy man." (A career Navy man leaves the Navy, but the Navy never leaves the man.) "What did you do in the Navy during WW II?" I asked.

"Oh, I had a bit of a tough go." He stopped briefly to take a few deep breaths. "I was a gunner's mate on a Fletcher class destroyer. The ship was sunk during the battle for Guadalcanal. The Japanese pulled me out of the water and I and spent the war in a prison camp."

"Oh really? Which one?"

He was clearly surprised at my interest. "Shinagawa. I rotted there until August of 1945. The place was a notorious hell hole. Have you ever heard of it?"

In stunned amazement, I stood back and took a deep breath. I replied, "My dad had been captured by the Japanese with the fall of Corregidor in April, 1942. He was also shipped to Shinagawa. Did you know him?"

George perked up at the question. "What was his name?"

"Lieutenant Jim Davis."

George then leaned over and squinted at my name tag, "Dr. Christopher Davis, Emergency Medicine."

George, with his hand shaking, leaned over and tugged the sleeve of my white coat and then told me the story of how, in 1942, in the Shinagawa prison camp, the Japanese guards had suspected George of stealing food. Four of them took him outside and proceeded to beat him with clubs with the plan to kill him. George thought that the guards intended to make an example of him to the other POWs.

With a tremor in his voice, he told me, "I remember it like it was yesterday. These Japs were beating the crap out of me when Lt. Davis came flying out of his tent and jumped into the fight. He was known to be a tough Irishman. He felt that my fight was his fight too. I guess because Lt. Davis was the ranking officer in the camp, the Japs decided that they could not kill me and not kill him too. They cursed at us and stomped away, leaving our bruised and bloody bodies in the dirt."

George then gently lifted his oxygen mask slightly and whispered to his wife, "Delores, can you believe it? My life has been saved twice. First by a brave young Navy lieutenant and then again, nearly 60 years later, on the other side of the world, by his son the doctor."

George's words brought my dad into sharp focus. He grew up without a father; his own dad was killed in a construction accident when he was four. He attended one of those iron-gripped all-boys Catholic high schools in which the emphasis was not on quality of education but discipline. Beatings at the high school were common. Selected for the Naval Academy in 1930, he graduated near the top of his class. As he described the Naval Academy in those days, the school was permeated with an Old South culture. Irish Catholics and Jews stood at the bottom of the social hierarchy. After graduation, he spent a few years as a gunnery officer aboard the cruiser "Pensacola." He met my mother in a Catholic-Catholic set-up and fell in love. He then decided to go to engineering school and earned a MS. My parents were married in 1939. My mother was pregnant with my older sister when Dad was sent to the Philippines before WW II. She did not see him again until he returned from the Shinagawa POW camp in 1945. Returning emaciated despite three weeks of Navy chow, he was granted 30 days' leave and was sent to his next duty station. For years thereafter, other naval officers would treat him dismissively because he had "missed" the Navy's huge battles with the Japanese.

My parents had three more children in rapid succession for a total of four. Dad was at a loss as to what a good father might be like. He loved to repeat the old Navy saying, "If the Navy wanted me to have children, they would have issued them to me."

When George spoke with such gratitude about my dad, my difficult relationship with my father flashed through my memory. His parental value system was obsessed with discipline. After all, that's what drove the Navy. In the military, officers and enlisted men do not mingle socially. Building on that model, dad and I never went together on any father-son outing such as a baseball game. He wanted me to be a success, but experience had taught him that manly toughness was a prerequisite. As he told me dozens of times, "Men are like steel. The only way to make them tough is to get them red hot and then pound the hell out of them." That is how he chose to raise his son. I could do nothing right and was always getting my ass chewed off in creative ways. One day, he told me to tidy the garage. I forgot. The following day, he asked me why I hadn't done what he had directed. I simply said that I had forgotten to do it. He then said, "Imagine you got the word that 200 marines were doing desert training and had run out of water. They reported to you that they needed water. Three days later, another group of marines found these young lads on the brink of death from dehydration. When the investigation started, the Navy came to you and asked you why you had not sent the marines their water. And you said, 'I forgot.'" My dad then turned and walked away. I was 12 years old. He wanted me to be tough; tutoring me in this way was the only way he knew how. As you can imagine, I developed a massive fear of failure. Having attended three high schools in four years, keeping a GPA in the 3.8-4.0 range all the way promised me a reliable escape pathway to college.

To his credit, his bravery and toughness became legendary in the engineering branch of the Navy. After his rocket ride up the career ladder, he was selected for admiral in 1960. In 1963, he was appointed the director of all Navy engineering efforts in the Pacific during the Vietnam War. The stress of that job crushed his sense of humor. Two glasses of bourbon helped. More than that, his Irish temper would start to rumble.

On countless occasions, my dad said to me, "I don't care if you love me. But you goddamn well are going to respect me." He was right on both accounts. I found him impossible to love, but I certainly respected him. He was smart, hard-working, the absolute standard for honesty and courageous beyond measure. Dozens of contractors for the Navy would try to cozy up to him and talk over a drink—or two—or more. Dad would only meet with them in his office and would never accept so much as a glass of water from any of them. I never could have survived 40 months of the physical and mental torture of the prison camp nor the pounding stress of being an admiral during the Vietnam War.

As I snapped out of my reflection on dad and our relationship, I realized George and Delores were wiping away their tears. I felt too moved to say a word…but, for the first time in years, I felt again that silent testimony of a lump in my throat.

George recovered steadily. After two days in the ICU at Montgomery General, he was well enough to be transferred to the Naval Hospital in Bethesda. I never saw George or Delores again.

My recollection of George's story was unexpectedly refreshed several years later by a discovery I made. In 1948, a former Navy surgeon wrote a memoir about his three years of imprisonment in Shinagawa. The book is entitled *Barbed Wire Surgeon* and, previously overlooked by me, had been collecting dust on our bookshelf for many years after my dad's death in 1992.

Thumbing through the book one afternoon, I found the following direct quotation from that book.

"Lt. Jim Davis....was captured and brought to Shinagawa. Here he continued to behave like a man and an officer who felt his responsibilities to his subordinate prisoner Americans. At the first sign of trouble, he was up on his feet protesting beatings that were prevalent in this camp when it was opened. He cajoled and argued with the Nip guards and noncoms in charge of the hospital. He physically intervened between men being beaten and guards doing the beating. He finally won their respect. The beatings dwindled away."[3]

---

3   Weinstein, Alfred A. (1948) *Barbed Wire Surgeon*. New York, New York: The Macmillan Company. p. 197.

Afterword

Would you like to be an emergency medicine physician?

Emergency Medicine as a specialty is a recent development. In the 1960s, physicians working in ERs were specialists in other fields of medicine and had no specific training in emergency care. As the number of ER patients swelled, chaos ensued. In time, hospital staff and administrators saw the urgent need to establish a corps of physicians properly trained to staff their emergency departments. The first residency program was started in 1970 at the University of Cincinnati. It established a reputation for graduating emergency medicine residents of extraordinary quality. This program became a beacon and the number of ER residencies has grown dramatically every year since; it now totals over 270 in the U.S. It took a while for this unfamiliar specialty to earn genuine respect from other physicians and surgeons. However, the critical role that ER docs played in bringing order out of dysfunctional ERs, and the vast amount of knowledge needed to handle emergencies of every kind, quickly enhanced their professional stature.

Physicians of every specialty must continually adjust to the fact that medical knowledge grows exponentially. The process of taking care of patients requires that physicians have a firm understanding of their specialty, have a meaningful relationship with each patient and conduct their practice in an organized and efficient manner. Except for ER docs, practicing physicians will usually spend their days seeing scheduled patients at a specified time to address a problem ideally within their area of professional expertise. To be sure, there may be nights on-call and weekend hospital rounds, but that physician has some ability to control the process. In order to practice effectively and efficiently, their day needs to be linear in that it is organized, scheduled and reasonably predictable.

Every day in the ER, however, is nonlinear. ER patients can pour in at any time, day or night. It is nonlinear because you may be caring for two to fifteen patients at the same time. It is nonlinear, as you may have a mixture of the critically ill mingled with several patient problems of no urgency. It is nonlinear because you do not usually have a previous relationship with the patient. Rather, you are meeting each patient anew and it is incumbent upon you to not only assess their medical needs but to size them up and determine the best way to establish rapport and trust with them as soon as possible.

Although these aspects of the ER role appealed to me, there were definite challenges and drawbacks with which I had to contend. As an ER doc, you are often consulting other medical specialists and, therefore, you face the possibility that your management of a particular case may be questioned or may become the focus of the inevitable hospital gossip. You may get push-back from a hospitalist who does not want you to admit the patient but assumes no responsibility for a bad outcome from refusing admission. You may get pushback from your spouse/soulmate who objects to the fact that your work week consists of three-quarters evenings, nights, weekends and holidays. You must attend that eighth-grade soccer match even when you are staggering with exhaustion. You worry as you see your associates try to resort to medications to help smooth out the awake/sleep roller coaster.

I particularly enjoyed being the leader of a team that was charged with caring for several patients at the same time with finite resources at any given time. The nurses, the techs and the administrative staff made up my team. By directing what needed to be done, I leveraged our operation enabling us to do more with less. The experienced nurses could fan out to speak with, treat and relate to the patients. In doing so, they were able to keep me out of trouble by identifying problems quickly. I loved being the quarterback of each shift in which, not only my medical skills, but my leadership talents were tested. Within this proving ground, I developed the sense of confidence that I could do the job properly. I ultimately came to trust that I had the physical and mental endurance to succeed.

Over the years, I also appreciated that in the ER, I developed a whole new diverse cadre of friends. They included doctors and nurses to be sure but also paramedics, police officers, technicians, pharmacists, educators and the patients themselves. When a specialist came in to see a patient in the ER, I enjoyed getting to know that physician and I used his/her expertise to teach me about the case. I befriended many police officers as our jobs are similar in so many ways. Like police officers, all clients (patient, witness, suspect, etc.) we ER docs have are unhappy that they need our help; the facts of a situation are often difficult to verify; the rotating shifts are exhausting; stress can come swiftly and without warning; decisions frequently have to be made quickly with inadequate information and will be second-guessed for years afterwards.

The variety of the cases every day stimulated me to review and learn about virtually every phase of medicine. Routinely, specialists in other fields would ask my opinion about cases outside their scope of training. I had to keep studying. I had to keep learning new information. Like many medical school graduates, I was a nerd and I thrived on managing a scope of practice that seemed to have no limits. I was never bored. What a great challenge!

A few years ago, after I had retired from the ER, I attended a dinner with seven of my former colleagues. One fellow made the off-handed remark, "If it weren't for my wife, I would not have any social life." The whole group enthusiastically jumped onto the subject and each one of us felt the same way. When we counted around the table, we discovered only one of the seven had been divorced. We all came to the same conclusion: one's happiness as an ER doc is not determined by where you trained or where you work; it is determined by whom you marry. After a quiet moment in the conversation, one fellow remarked, "My family is where I feel my deepest gratitude. I could not have survived the ER without my soulmate." We all agreed. My wife and I just celebrated our fifty-first anniversary.

I repeat here my favorite quotation from my dad that I mentioned earlier in the book: "The greatest gift a person can receive is the opportunity to perform meaningful work." The emergency department provides that opportunity.